Russell Harty was born in Blackburn in 1935, and as a boy he worked on his father's fruit and vegetable stall in Blackburn market. He won a scholarship to Exeter College, Oxford, where he read English, and then spent eight years teaching at Giggleswick, in Yorkshire, before taking a post at the City University in New York. In the mid-sixties he returned to England to produce 'arts programmes' for BBC radio and the programme *Aquarius* for London Weekend Television, for which he made his award-winning film on Salvador Dali. In the past two years he has established himself as a writer of some talent; but, above all, Russell Harty has become known for his successful chat show, *Russell Harty Plus*, for which he was awarded the Royal Television Society Award for the outstanding new male television personality of 1973.

Russell Harty Plus

First published in Great Britain in ABACUS 1974
by Sphere Books Ltd
30/32 Gray's Inn Road, London WC1 8JL

Published simultaneously in hardback by Elm Tree Books Ltd
90 Great Russell Street, London WC1B 3PT
Copyright © London Weekend Television Ltd 1974

Based on the television series from London Weekend Television Ltd
ISBN 0 349 11637 7

Set by Gloucester Typesetting Co Ltd.
Printed by James Paton Ltd., Paisley, Scotland.

CONTENTS

ILLUSTRATIONS

FOREWORD

'ONE minute there's no Russell Harty, and the next minute there you are, chatting 'em all up. Where've you come from, then?'

It's the word 'then' that I find most offensive. As far as I'm concerned, there's always been a Russell Harty and in the minutes before I wasn't chatting to people, I was walking alone, in gum boots and anorak, along a wide and empty Hebridean shore. I was summoned back to the house of my friends to take a telephone call from London. The programme was proposed, and as offers like that were not exactly coming in thick and fast with the Atlantic rollers, I accepted.

The biggest obstacle I had to face was the use of my own name. If I'd been called Mike Brown or Steve Smith, or something tough and easy and monosyllabic, I wouldn't have been so worried. But I'd only ever met one Russell before, and he was spotty and had red hair and bad teeth. And as for Harty, the kids I played with at school had never heard of Sir Hamilton, but they were able to make windy use of my name by substituting 'f' for 'h'. Now, two years after the programme first started, I'm irritated by the fact that people believe my surname to be 'Plus'. You can't win, and, if you could, it would be a matter of small consequence.

The chief joy of the programmes, and of doing them, is the journey one constantly makes into uncharted territory. Admittedly, I go into interviews with a deal of information about my guests – courtesy requires no less than that – but what I do not know is what human forces have been at work one hour, one day, one week before the meeting. I don't know whether the gentleman opposite has had a flaming row with his wife while he was shaving to come to the studios, or whether the lady with the beads of sweat is slithering into the first circle of the menopause, or whether this pop star has just been told on the telephone that his contract is about to be chopped.

Because of this constellation of hidden pressures and excitements, the interview can go any way. There is no such thing as an absolute final interview. This one is good, amusing, prickly, startling, sad. That one is flat, difficult and ultimately pointless. But no one – neither the producer, the director, the researcher nor the canteen lady – can offer any previous guarantee.

The circumstances that surround these interviews in the studio are equally without guarantee. The more it breaks out, the more I like it. The more consternation flooding over the face of the floor manager — the gentleman who controls the studio floor — the wider awake I become. One pop group, the Who, decided that their interview would work better if they each stripped the other's shirts off their backs. The drummer decided to strip down to his Y-fronts. Three or four distinguished guests, who included Frankie Howerd, Franco Zeffierelli and Rod Stewart, have taken my clipboard — my anchor, if you will, and thrown it behind the scenery. Danny Kaye turned the programme upside down thirty-seven seconds before we began by telling me backstage that he was going to introduce me as his guest and not vice versa. One famous American lady was taken short before we started and, not having time to go through three doors and two corridors, went instead in an ice bucket there and then. Do you wonder, therefore, that it happens *as* it happens?

The letters that come in are a constant source of surprise, amusement and worry: 'If I ever see you in the street, Mr Smarty-Harty, I'll smack your irregular teeth down your throat.' Maybe that what-I-take-to-be gentleman would be rendering a dental service. More difficult and infinitely more ambiguous is the lady who wrote to me saying: 'My parrot Joey gets a small erection every time you appear and I think you are getting better.' Some people make use of the most extraordinary yardsticks to measure success withal.

Perhaps it's easy to sit opposite the world's most glittering people and let some of the gilt rub off their gingerbread on to you. Certainly the waves of affection from the audience, and the obvious knowledge you have about people's achievements make you believe you inhabit, however temporarily, another special world. But we live ultimately in a world of flesh and blood, and neighbours and bills and crises and launderettes and tempers and income tax. However much your head may float in glamorous clouds, your feet have to be clamped on the ground. I interviewed Johnny Weismuller, whose Tarzan was and is totally definitive. We left the studio together — he seven feet tall, broad-shouldered like an inverted isosceles triangle, white Olympic blazer, bronzed Miami face; me shorter, stumpier, paler. There was a kid outside the studio who'd heard of the legendary figure within. He came up to us with a pencil and an old envelope and, looking at us both, said, 'Hey — which one of you two is Tarzan?' God bless him!

It is in the very nature of television to be ephemeral. I have never been able to understand why its critics use this charge against it. No one would accuse the Forth Bridge for standing up—or a rose for withering. A part of what draws people to watch a rectangle of glass is the changing pattern of the pictures and the words. I'm happy that some of what has gone on in front of me, and provided pleasure for a lot of people, has been crystallised and preserved.

RUSSELL HARTY

FRANKIE HOWERD

(*applause*)

RUSSELL: Welcome back! Now, just about anybody who is anybody has been seen on television over the past week. They've either had their own shows or they've been guests on other people's shows. So we were fairly desperate to find some way of filling in the next twenty-five minutes, and it was only after flicking through our file of names in desperation, that we came up with the name of my next guest. So, ladies and gentlemen, bear with me if you will and welcome him, if you can, Mr Frankie Howerd.

(*applause; music*)

HOWERD: Happy New Year. Happy New Year. Happy New Year to all . . . except one.

(*audience laughter*)

What is this introduction which I didn't write? That wasn't what you were supposed to say at all. Wait a minute, I've got it all written down. Well, go on—talk! (*long silence*)

Now he's dumbfounded. Did you ever? Did you ever? Oh, I should say so.

RUSSELL: But you're not . . . look, it's Christmas time and we're in a happy mood and everything . . .

HOWERD: *Are* we? . . . Gay abandon. If you'll pardon the expression. . . . (*hoots of laughter*) It's all right. Don't get self-conscious, Russell. I like your tie—that's nice. Those old curtains have run up well, haven't they?

(*audience laughter*)

He means well, poor devil. Go on. I notice you've got me with my back to the audience. They can't see what I . . . Change places. They don't want to see you. Let's see me.

(*they change places*)

That's better. Oh, my dear. The knob . . . look at that! Phallic symbols everywhere. Look at that! (*indicating the microphone*)

RUSSELL: Now, are you more comfortable now?

HOWERD: Oh, I'm fine, yes. It's just that nothing's in its right place tonight.

(*shouts of laughter*)

You're sweating already, aren't you? Your make-up's dripping already.

(*shouts*)

RUSSELL: What I was going to say was. . . .

HOWERD: Russell, *do* say what you were going to say. I want you to feel free.

(*audience laughter*)

I'm working for free, so why shouldn't you feel free?

RUSSELL: What I was going to say was, ah . . . I don't know what the hell I was going to say. I was going to say . . .

HOWERD: Well, it's all down there – you should know.

RUSSELL: It's not. This is from another programme.

HOWERD: Oh I see . . . yes.

RUSSELL: 'Ask her if she's happily married,' it says here.

(*shouts of laughter*)

HOWERD: It *is* from another programme, yes. Dorothy Squires you're talking about, is it?

RUSSELL: That's right, that's right. Now, you are *not* unemployed, are you – despite what I said about you?

HOWERD: Well ah, no. Well, you *know* I'm not. I mean, actually I've been doing the pantomime at the London Palladium, so no, I'm not. Unemployed? We're doing twice daily there and I get there at 2 o'clock, two in the afternoon, every day except Sundays, when I'm at matins, conducting, of course. We're there at 2 o'clock and there isn't much time to go out during the tea-break, so I'm there till about 11 o'clock at night. So I never see daylight. I just sort of go in – it's all dark. I'm like a comic pit-pony. I never see . . .

RUSSELL: But then when you go home, do you go straight to bed when you go home?

HOWERD: Depends whose home I go to.

(*shouts of laughter*)

RUSSELL: Pardon me for breathing.

HOWERD: I find it difficult to pardon you for breathing, Russell, but I see what you mean. It's a season of goodwill to all. Where's the .camera? Hah, hah.

(*audience laughter*)

RUSSELL: I mean when you go home, does it take you a long time to wind down? Or do you have a drink and play a few records and have a few folks in?

HOWERD: Now . . . there's four questions there. What do you want me to answer first? If the folks are in, the rest follows. I have the drink and the records, yes. I do. But you see, the thing is, when you're working from say — well, most of the day — you look forward to a good nosh at night, after the show. So I go out after the show and have a meal when I get in about 11 o'clock. All the lights are going out everywhere and I'm going home to me steak-and-kidney pudding, or something. God willing. You see? But I usually sit up and read or play records or something, because it's difficult, as you know, to go to bed on a full stomach. I mean, I mean . . . *choose* whose it is . . .

(*audience laughter*)

There's a woman here with a man with a dirty laugh.

RUSSELL: What part do you play in this pantomime that you're in?

HOWERD: Well, we're doing *Jack and the Beanstalk*. Now, would you believe: Simple Simon?

(*audience laughter*)

You would, wouldn't you?

RUSSELL: In *Jack and the Beanstalk*?

HOWERD: Yes, *Jack and the Beanstalk* — Simple Simon. That's right. Ah, he's the one — well, he's simple. And his name's Simon.

RUSSELL: Do you wear anything special?

HOWERD: Clothes. Yes.

(*audience laughter*)

It's not full frontal, you know. My face is. It's full frontal face. Full frontal face, yes.

RUSSELL: But do you — is it a traditional pantomime?

HOWERD: Don't keep waving your hands. What's that — automatic semaphore? What are you doing? Just relax, just take it nicely now. You see, that's . . . ooh, you haven't got your corsets on, have you?

(*screams of laughter*)

Somebody's going 'uuugh' out there . . .

RUSSELL: Well, it's all me.

HOWERD: No, I'm sorry. I beg your — ladies, it *is* the season of goodwill to all!

RUSSELL: Look, what I'm trying to say is, is it a traditional panto-mime, or is it updated to the 1970s?

HOWERD: We-e-ll, what is a traditional . . . ? I wouldn't know, because I wasn't that old when there were traditional pantomimes.

RUSSELL: How old are you?

HOWERD: Pardon?

(*audience laughter*)

I'll tell if you will. (*Long pause.*) Go on then.

RUSSELL: (*mumbles*)

HOWERD: Well, I'm two years less than that.

(*shouts of laughter*)

If I may say so, you look ten bloody years more. It's this depraved life you lead.

RUSSELL: I live a very quiet, private life.

HOWERD: Ah . . . well, never mind. Well, in your case it's not surprising. Anyway, look . . .

(*shouts of laughter*)

No, the pill . . . come on, come on . . . The pills are wearing off!

RUSSELL: Well, by 'traditional', I mean do you have a principal boy standing with tights on, slapping . . . ?

HOWERD: Russell, don't do that . . . please. I mean, this is embarrassing. What are they going to think?

RUSSELL: I'm talking about a principal boy, who's normally a girl, who stands with tights on and slaps her thigh and says: 'Four thousand miles and still no sign of Dick.'

(*shouts of laughter*)

HOWERD: Look, let's keep out of your private life.

(*screams of laughter*)

Let's get back to our pantomime. Now this is not *Dick Whittington*. It's disgusting. I mean, it is outrageous. I mean, if this wasn't the season of goodwill to all . . .

(*audience laughter*)

. . . I wouldn't bother. Now, now . . .

RUSSELL: I want to know—now, come on . . .

HOWERD: What do you want to know?

RUSSELL: . . . how much, how much more vulgar you can be at the London Palladium in 1973 than . . .

HOWERD: Vulgar? I'm never vulgar. You've been vulgar tonight.

RUSSELL: I have been harmless and mild and gentle and generous, which I intend to remain.

HOWERD: Ah, good. Generous!—that'll be the day.

(*audience laughter*)

RUSSELL: But it's twenty years since you played it last time, isn't it?

HOWERD: No, it isn't *twenty*. Since I played in pantomime?

RUSSELL: At the Palladium, at the Palladium.

4

HOWERD: Yes, well, actually the first play—the first pantomime I did was also *Jack and the Beanstalk* at the Lyceum Theatre in Sheffield. Now that was a long time ago. It was in (*mumbles inaudibly*) . . . and then I played in *Cinderella* as Buttons, and I've been in *Dick Whittington*. That's where the Dick came in—in *Dick Whittington*. Except that I was Idle Jack in it, you see. And . . .
(*audience laughter*)
And . . . I very rarely came into contact with Dick in the show at all.
(*screams of laughter*)
Not that I want to boast, but . . . I must say this is lovely. It's a marvellous New Year, isn't it, really? And me taking matins, I mean, on a Sunday. No, but ah . . . what else have I done? Oh, *Puss in Boots*. I did that a couple of times. And ah, there was no puss in that . . .
(*audience laughter*)
Or Dick. There was ah, there was . . . Do you mind leaving, please? Kindly leave this hangar. These studios get tattier every time, don't they?
RUSSELL: Listen, we are in the middle of a crisis. You know that, don't you?
HOWERD: Yes, yes indeed. We are, yes, we are at the moment . . .
You see, he's run out of questions. Get on with it. Get on with your list.
RUSSELL: I mean, we're talking about deprivation. You say it gets more kind of warlike every time you—I mean . . .
HOWERD: I said what?
RUSSELL: You said it's like a hangar. You said . . .
HOWERD: You said 'got more warlike . . .'
RUSSELL: Like . . . in the war.
HOWERD: Oh, how are you spelling 'war'?
(*audience laughter*)
RUSSELL: It's more *war*like—three-letter word.
HOWERD: Oh, it's a *three*-letter word. I see. All right. This gets more warlike. You mean the studio? London Weekend? Or do you mean . . . or what?
RUSSELL: No, I mean the conditions under which we're now living: that is fuel crisis, energy crisis, heating crisis, rail crisis. . . .
HOWERD: Yes, yes . . . keep on, do keep on.
(*audience laughter*)
RUSSELL: I really want to know how these things are affecting you deeply.

HOWERD: They're affecting me the same as everybody else. I mean, I know you won't believe this, but I am *human* and if it's cold I get cold and if there's no petrol I have to walk and it's just the same as for everybody else. Yes, you won't believe this. Actually, I'll tell you something—I enjoy walking. It's the one form of exercise I enjoy. Luckily, if the worst comes to the worst, you see, being at the London Palladium, I don't live all that far from it, so if the worst comes to the worst, I can at least walk through Hyde Park . . .

(*audience laughter*)

RUSSELL: I sometimes spend my lunch-hours in Hyde Park.

HOWERD: What you do in Hyde Park's *your* affair.

(*screams of laughter*)

RUSSELL: Now, I know from time to time you've mentioned in odd articles that you've done that it's a bit of a strain . . .

HOWERD: What do you mean—*odd* articles?

RUSSELL: *The* odd article . . .

HOWERD: Oh, that's better.

RUSSELL: . . . that has been written about you, that you find it a bit of a strain wandering about the streets, walking as you said, you like walking . . .

HOWERD: I do *not* walk the streets.

(*audience laughter*)

RUSSELL: *When* you're walking the streets . . .

HOWERD: *When* . . . yes.

RUSSELL: . . . that people sometimes think that they have proprietorial rights over you, that you're not being a funny man in the middle of the street, doing whatever you do do in the middle of the street.

(*audience laughter*)

HOWERD: The man's a twit, isn't he?

(*audience laughter*)

I was with you until you got to 'proprietorial'. After that I lost you. Now what did you mean by that? Be more explicit.

RUSSELL: Sometimes when you go to buy a newspaper . . . you with me so far?

HOWERD: Yes, that much, yes.

RUSSELL: Right. You've bought your newspaper, you turn round, you're going back home. It sometimes happens that people shout at you in the streets.

HOWERD: Yes, this is true. No, no, I know what you're trying to get at. No, the thing is, you see, that people—you once said to me, I

6

think, 'Do people expect comedians to be funny all the time?' And I said I didn't think people expect you to be funny. But I think what people expect – and they are disillusioned if you're not – is that you should look happy, or jolly. And now it's unfortunate – no, it isn't unfortunate – where's the – is this the camera I'm on? – No, you see when I'm going down low, you can see bags here, you see. Now there, you don't see them, but here you do.

(*audience laughter*)

Now you see 'em, now you don't, you know. Now the thing is if you're inclined to be at all 'baggy', if you'll pardon the expression, it makes you look melancholic. Now, my face has been compared to every known part of every known animal by critics – a tired camel, and a weary-looking potato and all sorts of things, and other vegetables as well. And now, if you're going down the street, you see . . . and a man said to me tonight, as a matter of fact – I was going into the London Palladium to rehearse – cold morning, and I was thinking: 'Now, when I get in there, I've got that to do, and there's some Press people there . . .' And the man said: 'Come on, cheer up, what's the matter with you?'

Now, I wasn't feeling unhappy, but the fact I have rather a melancholic face . . . I can't help this, it's just one of those things I'm born with . . . So unless I'm actually going round going . . . (*grins broadly*) I look rather miserable.

Once, I'd been to Wimpole Street to have a tooth fixed, and I was in agony when I came out of this dentist, you know, and I looked quite drawn, and this man said to me: 'Come on,' he said, 'What's the matter with you?' he said, 'You're paid to make us laugh. What's the matter with you? You look bleeding miserable.'

Now, it's true, and it's sometimes a little difficult to say: 'Well, I've got awful toothache and I could strangle you.' You know. And that's the thing with comics – not so much that people expect you to make them laugh all the time, because I don't think anyone expects that. But I do think people like to see you looking happy. It's very difficult actually, with the weather and sometimes the news, to go round going 'Ha ha ha' at nothing in the street. People usually think you're trying to pick 'em up if you do that.

(*audience laughter*)

So it's best to look miserable.

RUSSELL: Has anybody ever described you as a sex symbol?

(*audience laughter*)

HOWERD: Well, funny you should say this because . . . no, I *have* been so described actually as a sex symbol. . . . Go on, say something.

RUSSELL: By whom?

HOWERD: Me.

(*audience laughter*)

You want any more evidence?

RUSSELL: Yes.

HOWERD: No, well I'm not showing you.

No, I'm not a sex symbol. No, I'm not. I wish I was. No. I mean, they talk about the permissive society, but nobody permits me very much, I tell you that.

RUSSELL: Are you kept on a tight rein?

HOWERD: Er . . . tight rein? No, I don't—what do you mean, a tight rein? No, I just—no, I'm very—no, I don't think so. Are *you* a sex symbol?

RUSSELL: (*breathes heavily*)

(*audience laughter*)

HOWERD: Ask a silly question—now, let's face it! All right, tell me. Are you a sex—are you kept on a tight rein by who, and where is it the rein's tied round?

RUSSELL: My foot.

HOWERD: Your foot?

RUSSELL: Yes, my leg. My leg. No, we're here to talk about Mr Howerd . . .

HOWERD: Oh, you mustn't. (I thought we'd never get back to it.)

(*audience laughter*)

RUSSELL: Or to talk about three of the things that you won't talk about . . .

HOWERD: What's that?

RUSSELL: Which is money, politics and religion. Said he beforehand: 'I don't want to talk about money, don't want to talk about politics or religion . . .'

HOWERD: And I haven't.

RUSSELL: But why? Why do you put these stipulations down?

HOWERD: Why? Well, money—because I think that talking about money and what people earn is in bad taste for a start. And the average actor—well, the average Equity rate isn't very high . . . about 20 quid a week. It isn't as much as one would think, and actors and actresses and singers and dancers actually only get paid when they work, you see. So I don't think it's very tasteful.

I think that the thing about politics is, some people feel very strongly that they have a cause. I prefer to be—if you'll pardon the expression—neutral. That is to say, by not aligning myself in public with any particular party. Then I'm free to take the mickey, if you'll pardon the expression (I could put it stronger than that), out of them all. I think that's better for me. Somebody said to me: 'You know, you're a moral coward. You should come out and you should say what you think about things.' And I said: 'Well, I agree, a lot of people can do this and perhaps should do it if they feel so inclined. But as much as you want players, you also want a few umpires, a few referees, who don't take sides, but can adjudicate.' So by not coming down on one side, I can take the mickey out of everybody. And in any case, I'm a twit, and I don't know anything about it anyway. So that covers politics. And the last one is—what was the other one?

RUSSELL: Religion.

HOWERD: Oh well, religion is a very tricky question, which I would have thought didn't need asking because I mean, you can so easily offend people, and I think that's a private thing also. Let me just say one thing to you, about politics. People often ask me, 'Who are my favourite comedians?, and I always say, I always say . . . no, I don't say anything very much. I waffle like I'm doing now. Now, the thing is, when I first started in my career, I was up in Morecambe, and they had a beauty contest and forty girls were lined up and they said to me, 'Would you choose the beauty queen?' So I thought—I was very flattered—these beautiful girls all lined up in bathing suits and what not, you see—bikinis and things—so I marched along and they were all very beautiful, and I thought to myself: 'Who am I going to choose?' So I thought, 'Well, I'll—there's a dark-haired girl there. That's Miss So-and-So.' So I went back.

Now, as I came back from this long line-up of these forty ladies, I suddenly felt thirty-nine pairs of eyes, full of hate, on me: all those that I hadn't picked. Then I looked in the audience and I saw all the relatives of those that I hadn't chosen glaring up at me. And I realised I'd lost about—at least a hundred fans in one fell swoop. So therefore I thought, 'Never again!' I will never choose one. I don't mind crowning them, if you'll pardon the expresion, so to speak. That was an awful experience I had there once, mind you. I had to put a thing—a sash—round a lady's thing and this sash had—you know, you put the sash over and this sash had a safety pin. And I found that all of her wasn't all of her.

(*audience laughter*)

9

And there was a hissing noise. It was very embarrassing. So really, I found in future, I thought to meself, 'Don't. Let somebody else do the choosing and I'll go and crown them and do the charm and be lovable. But I won't be responsible for the decisions. I'm a coward you see, a moral coward. But I think the duty of an entertainer is to entertain and try and cause as little offence as possible, and try and make as many people happy as possible, and try and entertain as many people as possible. And not to get involved with a lot of controversy, unless they feel morally bound to do so.

RUSSELL: Right, right.

HOWERD: That's the end of the monologue. Yes, but after all, it is the season of goodwill to all. Where's the camera?

RUSSELL: Yes, it is.

HOWERD: It is—well, you know that I've done *my* best—God only knows!

RUSSELL: We're just on the edge of the New Year, and we must bring this to a close. Do you have a goodwill message for the nation?

HOWERD: For the nation? I've got a goodwill message . . . I've a message for London Weekend Television to say that . . . Look, Michael Parkinson is free next year . . .

(*audience laughter*)

Rush and grab him immediately!

I have a message for you to say that if you're going to invite guests like myself, would you please pay them something in future, and not just rely on a few brandies round the back there? And whatever I say to the nation, whatever goes wrong, we can always say 'Up Britannia!' and if one feels miserable, say 'Up the lot!'

(*audience laughter*)

You know, it's the best advice I can give, anyway.

(*applause*)

BARBARA CARTLAND

RUSSELL: Welcome back. Whatever the ups and downs of life, and whether we're in or out of the money, some things never change — ladies and gentlemen, Miss Barbara Cartland.

(*music; applause*)

BARBARA CARTLAND: Good evening.

RUSSELL: If you were staying at home this evening, would you be dressed in the same radiant fashion?

BARBARA CARTLAND: Not if I was alone at home. But I should still be very well dressed, because I dress to amuse myself, not entirely to amuse you and other men.

RUSSELL: But if you were to be alone, what would you be wearing?

BARBARA CARTLAND: Oh, something very glamorous . . . because everything I buy is glamorous. I like to feel glamorous. I think women should feel glamorous and it doesn't always depend on money — you can really make yourself look very glamorous with a gay piece of material, a pretty colour and still look a woman.

RUSSELL: And how do you think we poor and humbler men should make ourselves presentable?

BARBARA CARTLAND: Well, I think you should cut your hair a bit shorter . . .

(*audience laughter*)

RUSSELL: I should?

BARBARA CARTLAND: Well, not particularly you — say, men as a rule. Some of them look rather nice because they look Georgian, which is particularly my period in books. But if they're going to wear very long hair, then they ought to wear doublet and hose. Nothing looks more idiotic than long dandruffy hair on top of a pin-striped suit. . . .

(*audience laughter*)

Incidentally, if you take Vitamin A, you won't have dandruff.

RUSSELL: You're very hot on the vitamin bits, aren't you?

BARBARA CARTLAND: If you mean that I think they're absolutely wonderful and we can't live without them — yes.

RUSSELL: Well, how did people go on in what you call 'the olden

11

days'? They weren't pumping vitamins into themselves, were they?

BARBARA CARTLAND: In our grandfathers' day, the top soil, which grows all the goodness into the crops, was twelve foot deep. Today there's no top soil left. It comes as chemicals out of a bag. That is what's wrong. We're over-chemicalised . . . which has poisoned the soil – this is what all the excitement is about. We have terrible pollution on the land which has been done by pesticides, aerosprays, and DDT, which have been poured onto our soil and goes into the sea, which is also poisoned.

RUSSELL: But do you not recognise a small paradox in the sense that, if on the one hand you are taking all your pills and have bottles of them, you're doing that on one hand, and on the other hand, getting changed in the evening and putting on your maquillage . . . is that what you call it – maquillage?

BARBARA CARTLAND: I don't but *you* may. People have done that since the beginning of the world. Cleopatra made up her eyes because she wanted to look attractive, fashions change, beauties change with the fashions, and every generation does something which they think looks attractive.

RUSSELL: Do you not think that there is a paradox in making yourself look very pretty and glamorous as you undoubtedly are, on the one hand, and stuffing pills into yourself on the other?

BARBARA CARTLAND: It's stuffing the vitamins, not pills, into me that makes me feel so well, that makes me look, as you say, pretty – thank you very much – and makes me feel I can do things. I can work.

RUSSELL: Do you work very hard?

BARBARA CARTLAND: Well I've just, this last year, written nine books, because I've been taking the new brain pill, and I feel wonderful, wonderful, wonderful . . .

RUSSELL: The *new* brain pill?

BARBARA CARTLAND: Yes, it's just been produced. The Danes are making it and it is powdered brain. You take it with vitamins and you feel *so* wonderful. This is quite serious. Doctors are experimenting with it with retarded children and old people with the most tremendous results.

RUSSELL: But you make it sound grotesque. Can you imagine getting up in the morning and saying, 'Come on, darling, get your powdered brain!'?

(*audience laughter*)

BARBARA CARTLAND (*also laughing*): You just try it. I've brought you some. You'll feel absolutely wonderful. My son, who's obviously quite young, says he's never felt better in his life. My mother, who is ninety-five, says that she feels wonderful. She's absolutely marvellous.

RUSSELL: And is she on the powdered brain as well?

BARBARA CARTLAND: Oh yes. It's just saved her life. She was terribly ill in October, but now she says, 'I've never felt so well.' The only tragedy is, she was driving her car up till the 1st December and she really was very ill, and so we said, 'Darling, I do think you ought to give up your car.' And she gave it away, but now she's miserable and thinking of buying a new one . . .

RUSSELL: Good heavens! . . . What about the dependence that you have on these kind of things that you take? If they were all taken away, or you lost the key of the cupboard, or you were cast on a desert island without them, what would happen to you? Would your teeth and your hair drop out and everything go wrong?

BARBARA CARTLAND: I dare say I should get very much older rather quicker. That's all. It's as easy as that. Every vitamin that I take today is a natural food . . . It's condensed. It's exactly the same as what astronauts take going to the moon. You don't complain about that. *They* have a beefsteak in a capsule. Well, *you* can have a beefsteak in a capsule.

RUSSELL: But that's only because you can't take steak and chips to the moon . . . you can't sit there and have a four-course meal.
(*audience laughter*)

BARBARA CARTLAND: But you can have a four-course meal *and* you're still not having enough vitamins. Shall I give you an illustration?

RUSSELL: If it's pithy.

BARBARA CARTLAND: A man—to be a good lover—needs eighty grams of protein a day . . .

RUSSELL: I'd better write all this down.

BARBARA CARTLAND: Now, the average helping of roast beef is seventeen grams, so girls, you've got to start cooking.

RUSSELL: In your autobiography, I was amazed to read that you were rather angry about not being given an award at the end of the war.

BARBARA CARTLAND: That was a joke. I said I ought to have been a Dame, because I'd produced wedding-dresses and cami-knickers for the women in the Forces. Everybody took it quite seriously and wrote and told me how disgraceful it was to be asking for an award. That was meant to be a joke. In future, when I write an autobiography, I shall put 'joke' in the corner, rather like the man who puts up his hands that say 'clap', because really, people are so stupid.

RUSSELL: I, er . . . Thank you. I think you would have been a grand Dame. You have all the looks of a good Dame.

BARBARA CARTLAND (*abashed*): Now that really is the worst insult I've had, it sounds just like something at the pantomime!

(*audience laughter*)

I actually am a Dame at the moment, because I have been made a Dame of St John of Jerusalem. I work very hard for—the St John's Ambulance Brigade, the *most* wonderful organisation in the world and, after thirty years of hard slog I really think I've deserved that too. They've made me a Dame, but you see, it isn't a Dame in the sense that you call yourself 'Dame'. It does really sound so terribly like Mother Goose, doesn't it?

RUSSELL: You obviously didn't have a bad time in the war, did you? In your autobiography you make it sound as though it was a riot from start to finish.

BARBARA CARTLAND: Oh no! the war was for me a very unhappy time, because both my brothers, whom I adored, were killed at Dunkirk. But I felt that I had to do something important and was offered the job of Chief Lady Welfare Officer for Bedfordshire. Bedfordshire, being the centre of England, had all the really secret stations. Then all the girls who worked there came to me and said, 'I can't be married in these ghastly bloomers. How can I be? You know, I shouldn't feel married.' So I went to the War Office, and said to the Generals, who were women themselves, 'Could I have some more coupons for the girls in the Services?' and they said '*No*', with absolute pleasure. So then I said, 'I might be able to buy wedding dresses without coupons.' And they said, 'You must have a very trusting faith in human nature if you think you can get anything without coupons . . .'

RUSSELL: Right.

BARBARA CARTLAND: I thought, 'Damn them, I will.' So I went off and advertised in the local papers and, you know, it's absolutely fascinating, because every woman spends more money than she can afford on her wedding dress . . .

RUSSELL: Right.

BARBARA CARTLAND: . . . and she wears it once. Then it's put away in lovely tissue paper in a drawer and it's full of dreams, and she never wears it again. So I managed to buy, by the end of the war, a thousand white wedding dresses mostly for the A.T.S., some for the W.A.F.S. and one or two for the W.R.N.S., and I started the pool of white wedding dresses at the War Office, so that they could hire them for the day, and have a white wedding, which means such a *tremendous* amount to every woman . . .

RUSSELL: Your novels are all to do with romance, aren't they?

BARBARA CARTLAND: . . . Well, my fiction is, of course, and the amusing thing is that suddenly, I've become top of the pops because I've always written the same sort of book.

RUSSELL: Right.

BARBARA CARTLAND: I like virgin heroines. I like terribly glamorous things. I don't like people getting into bed without the ring on the finger—I don't think it's glamorous. I've always written the same sort of book and I've always sold very well. But suddenly, because people are fed up with pornography, they go out and buy Barbara Cartland; and I sold seven million paperbacks over the world last year—

RUSSELL: Right.

BARBARA CARTLAND: And in America, I'm billed as the greatest romantic author on earth. Don't tell the Brontës, will you? All over the world, I think we're getting back to romance. Gradually people are getting so bored with pornography that I'm told, in Copenhagen, all the worst places are closing down. The jets are ceasing to fly in. Instead, people sit at home and read me. It's much better for them!

RUSSELL: Barbara Cartland, thank you very much indeed.

(*applause*)

GARY GLITTER

RUSSELL: Once upon a time there was a singer called Paul Raven, and nobody paid any special attention to him. Then he changed his name and his image, stitched a few sequins on his suit and he was on his way again. Last week he released a new record. Just twenty-four hours later it was No. 1 in the Hit Parade—something only the Beatles and a couple of others have managed till now. Ladies and gentlemen, Mr Gary Glitter.

(*applause*)

GLITTER (*giving a jacket to Russell*): Christmas comes but once a year. I hope this jacket does as much for you as it did for me. That was the first one and you've got to wear it to all your parties, right?

RUSSELL: Can I—Can I have a look at it now?

GLITTER: Take it—I want you to put it on, Russell. Get it on . . . The game's up. That was a really nice jacket about a year ago. Look at it.

RUSSELL: Wait a minute, hold it. Is it going to fit? Am I going to look a lunatic if I put this on?

(*audience laughter*)

GLITTER: You're the same size as me, around the chest anyway.

(*Russell puts on jacket: cheers and applause*)

RUSSELL: This is a serious, intellectual programme.—Look at me. When you've given a whole concert do—do you feel tired, weary?

GLITTER: Oh yeah. I mean, sometimes I really do break down at the end of a concert. I mean, I sweat a lot. Or should we say 'perspiration' on your show?

RUSSELL: Or 'glow', if you so wish. . . . When you go to your dressing-room afterwards, are you on a terrific high though, if it's been a good [show]?

GLITTER: Yeah. I mean, I usually know if I've done well. However, I'm never satisfied. I'm a bit of a showbusiness 'ham' in so much as I'm—I'm a perfectionist. I *love* the business, I love working, and I'm always looking for new ways, something new to do.

RUSSELL: But—with a live show, I mean like the one you're doing,

16

you can't go back and make it go right, can you? I mean – if you've made a mistake, or something has gone wrong, if the people come in at the wrong time, you've had it.

GLITTER: That's right. Right.

RUSSELL: It upsets you if that happens?

GLITTER: Oh sure.

RUSSELL: Now, let's get down to the sequins bit. Where did you rumble the fact that if you covered yourself in sequins it might make an impression?

GLITTER: The thing was that I've been around for about thirteen years as a professional singer, right? And I wrote a song with Mike Leander, my co-writer/manager, and he said, 'Look, you've been around a long time. The Establishment know you quite well. Why don't you change your name?' So eventually we found the name of Gary Glitter.

RUSSELL: You went through quite a few names before?

GLITTER: Oh yeah, hundreds and hundreds.

RUSSELL: Tell us a few of the names.

GLITTER: It could have been Terry Timpson, or . . . Horace Hydrogen, or Vicki Vomit – that was one they threw up at the last moment. Terrible . . .

(audience moan)

RUSSELL: Unrehearsed – unrehearsed . . .

GLITTER: What have you got on your script there, you know? You haven't got a script, have you? You've got lots of . . .

RUSSELL: I've got a few notes that will remind me of the glorious things that you've done in your past.

GLITTER: Oh. Remind *me*, can you?

(audience laughter)

RUSSELL: Like, you're no longer married now, are you?

GLITTER: No. No. Unfortunately . . .

RUSSELL: Was that a depressing scene for you?

GLITTER: Not really. I got married when I was nineteen, and I think nineteen is too young for a man to get married. He's still a boy. I'm still a boy, and I'm still looking . . .

(audience laughter)

RUSSELL: And slightly older than nineteen you are.

GLITTER: I'm er – much older than nineteen, yeah.

RUSSELL: But somewhere between one and one hundred.

GLITTER (laughing): Well, actually I'm fifty-two, but I'm wearing well. I think so, anyway . . .

RUSSELL: What I want to talk about now is . . . you're now something very big in the pop scene with the whizzing-up-Number-One bit . . . Therefore, do you have a great many pressures that you haven't had to resist before, like when you were trying to make it? Or are you protected by managers, and arrangers, publicity people?

GLITTER: Not *protected* — you know, not wrapped up in cotton wool, but when I really get down to working hard I really don't see what's going on. I read all the letters and things I get, you know.

RUSSELL: Do you get any 'hate' mail?

GLITTER: No, I don't, which is always amazing. Always amazed me anyway.

RUSSELL: Do you have an extremely good manager who filters the 'hate' mail to one side, so you don't see it?

GLITTER: Maybe. I don't think so though.

RUSSELL: Do you have any hero in the pop world?

GLITTER: I suppose everybody who grew up at the same time as I did, which is — I left school in 1960 so I suppose Presley was the King — he was one of the . . . one of the people that I looked up to. However, I looked up to Jerry Lee Lewis and Little Richard and Chuck Berry. You know, I was like getting a tennis racket with a piece of string round it and trying to do a Chuck Berry. For a guitar, that was.

RUSSELL: In front of a mirror?

GLITTER: Oh yeah, always in front of a mirror.

RUSSELL: Yes. Mmm. Is a mirror a very important part of your life?

GLITTER: Well, I think a mirror is a very important part of everybody's life for one, and the other thing is that if you want to entertain you have to learn to express yourself.

RUSSELL: Right. Those salutes — those salutes that you have just been giving. . . . Aren't they almost Black Power salutes, those?

GLITTER: Er — I think they use it. However, mine should be really the peace sign. I mean, that's where I got it from, the peace sign.

RUSSELL: Not the Harvey Smith way round?

GLITTER: The Harvey Smith! (*laughs*)

RUSSELL: You didn't have the most — the happiest of childhoods, did you?

GLITTER: Well, my family moved around quite a bit. My mother re-married when I was eleven. I was born in Banbury in Oxfordshire, and then we moved to London, so I was a country boy that came to London, and er — used to speak with an accent which I can't remember how to speak.

18

RUSSELL: A country accent?

GLITTER: Yeah, and it was very, very difficult . . . like kids used to take – take the – er – out of me . . .

RUSSELL: The micky?

GLITTER: The micky, that's it. I was trying to think of it.

RUSSELL: I'm wondering what they would do to *me* if they saw me clutched in this tight suit.

GLITTER: I think you look very good, actually.

RUSSELL: How do you clean these sequins? (*pointing at his jacket*)

GLITTER: You can't. That's the whole point.

RUSSELL: You can't?

GLITTER: So you can just imagine, I've worn it about eight times . . . and I've been soaking wet and you're wearing it now.

(*audience roars with laughter*)

GLITTER: Just think of that. I mean, just think of the people that would really dig to do that though.

RUSSELL: What I'm thinking of is the lady in the launderette's face, when I turn up with this, this evening . . .

GLITTER: Well, I don't have to. Somebody does mine for me.

RUSSELL: . . . and see it going round in the spin-dryer. Now, you've been quoted as saying that you regard a lot of the music that you sing – a lot of the music you actually listen to, as pure mindless stomp.

GLITTER: Yeah. I'm not – er – I'm not saying my music is very clever. It's great music to join in with. It's great music to dance to. We made it purely for the discotheque audience point of view originally, and nobody was saying 'Oh yeah, this is really great introverted music.' I mean, it's just pure physical music, inasmuch as if you want to dance and bop around.

RUSSELL: Are you not afraid of the actual – the time span on it? In other words, that it's going to be out of fashion in four, five, six, seven weeks and then the next one comes up?

GLITTER: Er – not really, no. I mean I've been lucky for a year and a half now.

RUSSELL: When you're very tired and you're at the end of a gig, or at the end of a concert, how do you relax? How do you bring yourself down to earth?

GLITTER: Usually, we just have a few friends round. I can't really go out any more without being bothered quite a lot. I like being bothered, but I don't like, you know. . . . So we just play games, – er – I got lots of pin ball machines and . . . You must come over some time. I'll take some money off you.

19

RUSSELL: Shall I wear this when I come?

GLITTER: Er — you could do.

RUSSELL: The reason I was asking you how you relax is because I had heard — a little bird told me, that you spent a lot of time fishing.

GLITTER: Fishing is my hobby. However, I don't get a lot of chance to do it, but I love fishing. I love getting into those wellies and the — I mean, it's such a contrast.

RUSSELL: Yes. Oh quite. Yes. I do see. When you're sitting in your wellies . . .

GLITTER: Sequinned wellies . . .

RUSSELL: In your sequinned wellies, with your rod hanging out over the water . . .

(*audience laughter*)

RUSSELL: . . . waiting for the fish to bite, what do you make of Gary Glitter then, when you're in a quiet tranquil mood?

GLITTER: Well, quite frankly, you're so busy . . . do you ever fish?

RUSSELL: I have fished.

GLITTER: Well then, you'll know the answer to that one. I mean, you're so busy fishing and trying to get into what's going on below the water, right? that you don't think of anything. That's why it's good, so relaxing, very tranquil.

RUSSELL: Somebody taught me how to fish in Scotland.

GLITTER: Really?

RUSSELL: And they told me how to use a spinner, to get a trout in. And the first time I caught one I was so excited I couldn't believe it. I was so excited I wound the trout right up to the top of the rod, and I said to the guy who was teaching me, 'Well, how do I kill it?' and he said, 'Why don't you climb up the rod and stab it?'

(*audience laughter*)

RUSSELL: As well as sitting on your bank, you also listen to Beethoven, which is surprising.

GLITTER: Well, I think that music is . . . like a glass of wine. You know, for an example, I wouldn't dream of getting up in the morning and having a brandy first thing. So I'd have some pop music and some orange juice, and as you go through the day you end up by having, say, Beethoven, or even Carol King, or something more relaxing, and you take a brandy. Do you know what I mean? It's like having relaxed after-dinner music — right? — as opposed to raving it up all the time.

RUSSELL: Did you come to Beethoven late in life?

GLITTER: Yeah, I did actually. I didn't get it until I got to Germany.

RUSSELL: You make Beethoven sound like measles, a bit.

GLITTER: It is. It grows on you. I mean it's there, once you catch it you know, you've got it.

RUSSELL: Have you made a lot of money?

GLITTER: Yes.

(*audience laughter*)

RUSSELL: How do you intend to cater for your old age, for insurance, for when people no longer want to know who you are?

GLITTER: You see, I don't think anybody ever believes – an entertainer certainly doesn't ever believe that . . . they will no longer . . .

RUSSELL: That's a good answer.

GLITTER: You go along because you like working. That's the main thing. Once you forget that, then you're – the game's up.

RUSSELL: Um – I'm very envious of your chest, and I'm wondering how the hell I'm going to get out of this jacket.

GLITTER: Well, don't get out of it. Stay in it. I'm sure that your next guest is going to enjoy it as much as I've enjoyed looking at you.

RUSSELL: Right! Well, it's been a great pleasure talking to you.

GLITTER: It's nice talking to you.

RUSSELL: Good. Fine. That was Mr Gary Glitter.

(*applause*)

DAVID NIVEN

RUSSELL: Hello. Good evening, ladies and gentlemen. My guest tonight played the trombone and the drums in the band at school, where his nickname was 'Podger' and sometimes even 'Binge', whatever that may be. But he overcame all that and went out into the world to meet Barbara Hutton and Clark Gable and Humphrey Bogart and Errol Flynn, Elizabeth Taylor, and countless others who quickly counted him amongst their closest friends. He was one of the world's top movie stars over thirty years ago and he remains at the top steadily, today. He's flown in from his home in the South of France specially to be with us tonight. Ladies and gentlemen, Mr David Niven.

(*music; applause*)

Now, you've worked everywhere in the world, haven't you?

NIVEN: Well, in the last ten years I've worked in fourteen different countries. Not everywhere, but it's a lot. And I love it. I've got itchy feet, and I like to look around.

RUSSELL: Yes. Now despite the fact that you've worked in fourteen countries, you remain quintessentially English. I mean you look English, and your voice is English, and everything. Before we launch into the deeper parts of our conversation can we have a little *hors d'oeuvre* and see you at work as a quintessentially English man: one of the last of the few. There we are. You as one of the 'few'.

Excerpt from The First of the Few, *with David Niven as Crisp.*

First Pilot: *Station Commander, what's in the wind now?*

Crisp: *Oh, don't get up, please.*

Flight Lieutenant: *Good afternoon, sir. Was the C.O. hurt?*

Crisp: *Oh, nothing much. He's done something to his ankle, I think. I hear you chaps had quite a good bag this afternoon.*

First Pilot: *Yes. Six, sir.*

Crisp: *Six. Good, that makes twenty so far.*

Second Pilot: *Quite a picnic, sir.*

Crisp: *And a picnic for the Bosch too. Where's Titch?*

Flight Lieutenant: *Sergeant Jones saw him come down in the drink, sir. He got out all right, though.*
Crisp: *He can swim, can't he?*
First Pilot: *Yes, sir. You should have seen him at Brighton last year.*
Crisp: *I missed that little party.*
(aircraft noise)
Second Pilot: *Spitfires, chaps, just in case you've never seen one.*
First Pilot: *Can't see a 'Spit' in the air without getting a kick out of it.*
Second Pilot: *Why do you like it, old boy?*
First Pilot: *Can't help it. After all, it's my line.*
Second Pilot: *Whatever are you talking about? I thought you were a ruddy artist.*
First Pilot: *That's exactly what I mean.*
Third Pilot: *I agree with old Rembrandt. It is an artistic job.*
Crisp: *That's not surprising. It was designed by an artist.*
Squadron Leader: *Do you mean Mitchell, sir?*
Crisp: *Yes, R. J. Mitchell.*
Squadron Leader: *He was a wizard.*
Crisp: *You're right. He was a wizard.*
(*applause; laughter*)
RUSSELL: You can't get more English than that, can you?
NIVEN: You can't get more awful than that, either.
RUSSELL: How long is it since you saw that, do you think?
NIVEN: I haven't seen it since we made it. I had five weeks' leave during the war to shoot that, and it was supposed to be a picture of national importance because of the Spitfire thing which had just won the Battle of Britain – or was winning it then, with the Hurricane. I had five weeks' leave to do it, and those pilots you just saw, incidentally, were all Spitfire pilots, and we shot that on a fighter station during the Battle of Britain at Ringwood in Hampshire. Many of those fellows you saw were eventually killed. They'd do a scene with me, this fool, this Station Commander creature, and then they'd go up and do a sweep over France and come back. We did the whole thing there. But it's terrifying seeing an old movie. I've made eighty-seven now altogether – some were made thirty–thirty-five years ago, you know, and there've been certain physical changes. Everything seems to have fallen down or fallen out.
(*audience laughter*)
The worst happened the other day in New York. I was in an elevator and there was a very nice woman in it with me. She kept on looking

23

at me, and finally she said 'Pardon me, but weren't you David Niven?'

(*audience laughter*)

RUSSELL: Your life now, though, is not altogether acting. You do go about talking to people a lot, don't you?

NIVEN: Well, yes, I do. I go every year to America for five or six weeks and lecture.

RUSSELL: What kind of audiences do you have? Who turns up?

NIVEN: Well, that's the frightening thing—they change. I mean— one day it would be 2,400 blue-rinse ladies of the older group . . . then, the next night, it would be an audience of college kids from a university. Then a mixture of the two: townsfolk, and that sort of thing, and then dinner clubs. It's fascinating. It's frightfully difficult. . . . Had a little problem with the Mormons.

RUSSELL: Mormons?

NIVEN: I went to Salt Lake, and it's dry there, you know. I had two little bottles in my bag. I had a bottle of brandy, for obvious reasons, and a bottle of eau-de-cologne. The bottle of eau-de-cologne is for when you get frightened. You smell it. It's better to have a little eau-de-cologne. And the Mormons are really dry—nothing. And I got a little muddled, through fright, at the sight of two thousand Mormons and so I didn't drink the eau-de-cologne, but I did worse: I put the brandy under my arms!

(*audience laughter*)

NIVEN: Of course, they were convinced they had the king lush of all time.

RUSSELL: Can we jump back now down periods of history? I mean I shouldn't use the word 'history' about such a young-looking man, but can we go back right through your life to the early days. You did go to a lot of public schools. In your book, which we will come to eventually, you seem to have gone to a lot of private schools from which you left or departed rapidly.

NIVEN: Well yes, I did. I was sent away to boarding school at six which I think is cruelty to animals anyway. And the only people in the world to do that are—the laughingly so-called British middle classes and upper classes. Nobody else in the world. That's including the Chinese—oh, the Chinese *do*, I think. And it's torture if you go to the wrong one. Then it really was torture because this was just after the First World War, and a lot of the masters were sort of shell-shocked, strange creatures. We got badly bashed around, and bullied, and hung out of windows. It wasn't funny at all. And I was finally taken away from that. I persuaded my mother, who didn't quite get the message that it was awful, and was sent to a nice school which was too soft, and I bloomed like a rose there, you see, and I went much too far and got expelled from that one . . . And then I was sent to a school for bad boys which was really awful.

RUSSELL: Which was a school full of bad boys, as well?

NIVEN: Yes. Full of them, oh yes, absolute monsters. Many went to Borstal. It was a vicious ex-naval lieutenant commander who ran it, who thrashed us all the time. We split up into vicious little gangs for shop-lifting and that sort of thing.

RUSSELL: Shop-lifting?

NIVEN: Oh yes. Oh, we had to. We needed the extra chocolates, and this was no joke. I was much the youngest, and had a sort of innocent face, believe it or not, which they used – the rest of them. I was the one that would go and talk to the old lady who was running the shop, and ask if I could get some things for my poor uncle who was not feeling too well in hospital. While she was talking to me, making me feel better, the others were at it.

(*audience laughter*)

Then I used to have the bag of marbles. If anything happened in the big shops while they were taking a few things over there, I'd drop this bag, and everybody would run and help me. And I'd cry. I'm not a bit proud of this, I want you to know. I'm not a bit proud of it.

RUSSELL: You're corrupting the nation. I mean everyone watching tonight . . .

NIVEN: No, it's disgraceful.

RUSSELL: . . . will rush out with a bag of marbles.

But having gone through that kind of a schooling, you did eventually end up at Stowe, didn't you?

NIVEN: Yes.

RUSSELL: Under Roxburgh.

Everybody I've spoken to about Roxburgh, and I've read things about him, seems to be enchanted by him. What special magic did he have for you?

NIVEN: Well, he was an incredible man, and he took infinite pains with the tricky boys – which I suppose I was by that time, and he gave you confidence, he gave you authority, and he really saved my life. I think – I'm not joking – if he hadn't taken me into Stowe, I probably would have gone to Borstal, because I was going downhill at speed. In spite of the innocent face, I was going down. He was a

25

marvellous man, and he made a point of knowing every boy's christian name. It doesn't sound like much, but if you're rather insecure and had had a strange time, it meant everything for the Headmaster to call you by your first name. Never forgot your birthday. Obviously he had a little book, but he never forgot.

RUSSELL: You must meet millions of people in the course of your professional and public life. Do you keep a little book?

NIVEN: No, I don't keep a little book, but I think, first of all, you cannot be an actor unless you're an egomaniac – that's the first thing. Now, if you're an egomaniac, you want to be liked, and the whole thing about being an actor is you want to be liked. You've got on the stage and you want to be liked, so I think actors really play a little part for every single individual they meet. I'm sure that I'm behaving differently to you this minute, because I want you to like me, than I will to somebody I'll meet later on this evening.

RUSSELL: Now then, let's take you out of Stowe and away from Roxburgh. Why did you then elect to go to Sandhurst, which was a deeply disciplinarian kind of thing?

NIVEN: Well you see, I didn't choose it really. My mother chose it. My mother chose it because we were broke. First of all she chose the Navy for me, and I tried to get into the Navy but I got 8 out of 300 in mathematics . . .

(*audience laughter*)

. . . and so the Navy thought that I wasn't quite the man to be steering huge battleships. So, then I tried for the Army, and I managed to get to Sandhurst. And I was imbued with discipline there. My God you were. I really wanted to be a Field Marshal – it's unbelievable, but I did! I didn't get very far along the way, but I tried, I think, for a bit. But then you see there was no promotion in those days. I joined a Highland regiment in Malta. And it was sixteen years before you became a Captain, so there was this whole vista of horror stretching in front of me – and low pay. We got nine shillings a day as a Second Lieutenant, and you had to spend £150 on your uniform.

RUSSELL: Which you had to pay?

NIVEN: Oh yes, and that was pretty spooky because you got nine shillings a day, but you had unlimited credit because you were in what was laughingly called a decent regiment.

RUSSELL: All through your life you have managed to work out some method of self-preservation. You've never finally gone under, though you've always been in difficult situations. I'm thinking now of a

26

situation in Malta when you managed to preserve your dignity in a most extraordinary and extreme circumstance, not altogether unconnected with what's in that glass (*points to drink David Niven is holding*).

NIVEN: I know what you mean, yes. Well, this particular regiment had a strange theory that you were in a family – that you'd be in the regiment for your life. So the officers – when a new officer joined at eighteen and a half, you know – they didn't speak to you. They didn't bother about you at all, because they had your whole life. It was very depressing. But also they had a macabre idea that on the first guest night, the new officer would be the guest of the Colonel. Well, the Colonel had not spoken to me. Months had gone by and he never addressed a word to me. I found myself prepared to sit next to this strange creature at dinner, and I got very highly strung about the whole thing, and took heavily to the grog because whisky was six bob a bottle. I hacked away at that, and nobody was speaking to me very much at all. Then we go into dinner, and I'm the guest of honour sitting next to the Colonel. Just before we went into dinner, I realised that – I could get bleeped now, you know – that my bladder was bursting . . .

(*audience laughter*)

. . . and I was just about to disappear when we were marched into dinner. I'd got this tight, stiff collar on and everything, and nobody speaking to me, and then soup – cold soup came – more strain . . .

(*audience laughter*)

. . . then I started taking to anything. All this wine, thinking that it would work as an anaesthetic, you know, and take this dreadful pain away. I was absolutely dying, finally. You've no way – you can't say 'Please Sir, may I . . .' No way. So I thought 'Well, I'm going – my whole career is going to end in a pool underneath – underneath . . .

(*audience laughter*)

. . . underneath the mess silver and everyting. And at that moment the one friend I had did a genius thing. The mess butler came over and he whispered in my ear, 'Mr Trubshaw's compliments, sir. I've put an empty magnum underneath your chair.' Well, I mean that's a difficult game. That's a very tricky business. Very tricky business indeed, and I got it arranged . . .

(*audience laughter*)

. . . and was nonchalantly crumbling a biscuit with this hand, when this terrible Colonel turned to me – this man who had never spoken

27

to me — and said, 'I have pleasured women of every nationality and most animals . . .

(*roars of laughter*)

. . . but the one thing I cannot stand is a girl with a Glasgow accent. Pass the port.' And he never spoke to me again in three years. Very strange man.

(*audience laughter; applause*)

RUSSELL: Do you feel comfortable now?

NIVEN: I'm very happy now. Really happy.

RUSSELL: Now a lot of the things that you've written about in this astonishing book that you have produced are rakish, peculiar, some of them outrageous, and a lot of them at odds with the guy whom I find sitting in front of me. I mean, as I was saying earlier, you push things quite far. You bestow your masculine favours fairly liberally throughout the book, and then here you are, quintessentially English again. You know — upright, decently dressed, cuffs at the right length, nice moustache. How do you square yourself with this dichotomy?

NIVEN: Well, I don't know, you see. As I said before, if you're an actor, you have to be an egomaniac. Now, the supreme act of egomania is to sit down and write 130,000 words about yourself, isn't it, really? So when I decided to do that, I thought, 'There's no point in pulling the punches. No point in cutting out things that did happen.' You've got to go the whole way because that's what makes the picture. I had a few, very few, letters from people saying they didn't like the language, but you cannot write about whores and soldiers and actors without using four-letter words. There's no way. So there's rather too much of that maybe, and some of the stories, as you say, are pushing the limit a bit. But they happened, and I think it doesn't matter. I'm not a bit ashamed, and if it gives other people pleasure, or teaches some people things not to do, then I'm even happier.

RUSSELL: Do you ever feel that your life has become mixed up with your film work, so you can't distinguish the one from the other?

NIVEN: Well, I think this, you see, Russell. I think that, first of all, movie acting is entirely a type-casting business. If there's a great part for a Chinese laundryman they're not going to ask me to do it . . .

(*audience laughter*)

They'll get a Chinese, won't they?

RUSSELL: Right.

NIVEN: Right. So obviously I fit into certain categories and always did, and I've made a very nice and profitable career for myself out of playing officers, dukes and crooks really – with an occasional clergy-man which didn't fit! That sort of thing. I mean I've obviously been cast as that, so I suppose that's what my front is.

RUSSELL: Right. When you knocked on the Hollywood door, did you go with crooks and dukes and clergymen in your mind?

NIVEN: I went because I was absolutely destitute. I was in Holly-wood, I was broke, and I became an extra in westerns. I finally became registered as Anglo-Saxon Type No. 2,008 because I looked like that. But Hollywood, with its genius, immediately cast me as a Mexican.

(*audience laughter*)

So I did twenty-seven westerns as a Mexican, with a moustache and the hat and the blanket and all that. I was never allowed to speak of course with this voice. But then I got on. – Then I was playing cads.

RUSSELL: Did you have to audition for these things?

NIVEN: Well, you see, the thing about Hollywood then was that all the casting was done right there. The only way into Hollywood was right in Hollywood itself. There was no television then, so nobody was seen on the box and picked up by the producers. They brought out very few established actors from Broadway. Very, very few because it was five days on the train from New York to California, or twenty-seven hours in the air thudding into the Allegheny moun-tains in flames – a horrible trip at 5,000 feet. So they brought nobody out and they did the casting on the set. For instance if there was a director that needed a horse doctor, he would line up half a dozen young men who looked like horse doctors and then he would make each . . .

RUSSELL (*laughing*): What does a horse doctor look like?

NIVEN: Well, I don't know. And then each of them would have to say, 'I'm sorry, Madam, but your horse has diabetes . . .'

(*audience laughter*)

And then whoever said it best got the part. I remember Chaplin told me that the same sort of thing went on on Broadway. Charlie Chaplin was up for the part of the Fourth Soldier in *Henry IV*. The producer was a man called William Gillette, who was an awe-inspiring figure. He lined up eleven young actors – Chaplin was the smallest and right at the end of the line – and he said, 'Now, gentlemen, I shall say to each of you in turn, "The Dauphin is dead." Your reply to that is the one word "Dead?" Now, he who says that the best will become the Fourth Soldier in *Henry IV*.' Chaplin said he was petrified after six people had been dismissed. Every inflection he'd ever thought of had gone, and his mind was a blank. Finally, he was on the stage confronted by this huge man and he said, 'The Dauphin is dead', and Chaplin went 'Tch tch tch tch.'

(*audience roars with laughter*)

RUSSELL: But you did slip your cool once, didn't you? You had an audition with a guy called Curtiz?

NIVEN: He was from the old Reinhardt school in Germany. The Reinhardt school was to break actors down to putty, and then mould them into the fashion the director wanted, which is lovely for the director and hell for the actor. I was being tested with nine or ten other young men, all looking exactly the same, for a part in *The Charge of the Light Brigade*. We all had tight uniforms on, and it was 130 degrees and no air-conditioning and we all had to play the same scene with Olivia de Havilland for the test. I was standing there, and eight other actors who had played the scene had been dismissed in ignominy, and I'm wheeled on. Curtiz said, 'Where's your script?' and I said 'Well, I know it.' He said 'Where's the script?' I said, 'The actual bit of paper?' and he said, 'Yes. Where is it?' I said 'Er . . . in my dressing-room.' He said, 'Run and get it.' So I said, 'You ****** run and get it.'

(*audience laughter*)

And then he said, 'Dismiss the others. Give him the part.'

RUSSELL: Did people help you up at that early stage?

NIVEN: Well, Hollywood was extraordinary in those days. There was the minimum of bitchery and jealousy, the maximum of kindness and helpfulness. I was cast to play a part in a film called *A Feather In Her Hat* which even today I would sweat at the thought of, with the whole build-up based on 'Wait till Leo get's here.' Leo (that was me) comes in and falls on his face. It was a big party scene and it was the first scene I'd had to play. I had to wear white tie and tails and I hadn't got that – couldn't afford them. So I borrowed them from Herbert Marshall who was a great English actor. Poor man, he'd lost a leg in the First War, so his fly buttons did up the wrong way, like a woman's coat . . .

(*audience laughter*)

. . . for some reason, to get the cork leg in there, and I was so nervous that I couldn't get my fly buttons done up, and they had to send in a woman from the wardrobe department to do my fly buttons up with a button hook! I was outside the door waiting for the red light to signal me to come on and do my splendid bit. The director had rehearsed it two or three times and I was terrified with two hundred people there, and finally the light went on and I was on. I came on, tripped over the track, goosed some poor old lady by mistake . . . knocked things over, I don't know—somehow tottered through the scene . . . and everybody applauded. I thought—'It's easy, it's absolutely easy.' He said, 'David, that's great, that's absolutely marvellous. Do it again, exactly like that, don't trip over the thing, and mind the old lady's you know—but do it again exactly like that. We've got it in the bag. You're home. Fine.' I went outside, I couldn't wait for the red light to go on. Came on, sailed through it, and afterwards I discovered . . . friend of mine, one of the extras, told me that before the first take he came on the set and said, 'This boy—this is his first big chance, first big scene. Doesn't matter how bad the first take is, everybody is to applaud at the end. Then I'll put some film in the camera.'

(*audience laughter*)

Pretty nice . . .

RUSSELL: It's a very heartening story. . . . From that, an enormous leap in time again because of the exigencies of our time, to the night of the Oscars, the night that you won your Oscar — which you make a hair-raising, experience of when you write about it, because some fool had actually decided that you should be one of the compères of that great night.

NIVEN: I know. That was very tough. But the compères that night were Jack Lemmon and Bob Hope and me. And there you are—you're really up in front of the world you know. You see, in a way, it's basically fair that the Hollywood system of the Oscars is this: that the writers vote for the writers, the actors vote for the actors, the cameramen for the cameramen and so on, directors for the directors. Five people are nominated in each category and then the whole 5,000 members of the Academy vote for the winners, so it's a four to one shot anyway. You have to be ready with your 'brave loser' face, you know, or try not to weep or throw up or whatever it is . . .

RUSSELL: . . . or both.

NIVEN (*laughing*): Yes, both. And I was pretty highly strung and then, Irene Dunne it was, opened the envelope and read out the winner for the Best Actor—which is nonsense, really, because it's a team effort, isn't it?

RUSSELL: Right.

NIVEN: You're only having to say the words that some genius wrote. Up I got and my name came out, charged down the aisle—I thought she was going to change her mind . . .

(*audience laughter*)

. . . And fell—fell headlong up the stairs . . . crashed to the ground, and everybody roared with laughter, you know, and then Irene gave me the Oscar and the microphone and departed. And I thought, 'Well, I'd better try and explain this peculiar entrance.' So I said— 'The reason I fell down was . . .' I meant to say I was so loaded with good luck charms that I fell over, that I was top heavy. But I got as far as the word 'loaded' and—and they roared with laughter, you know, . . . and that was the end. I mean I couldn't top that. I was the only self-confessed drunk in the business.

(*audience laughter*)

RUSSELL: Now you've led your life in this total glare of publicity which is no less now than it was—say, twenty or thirty years ago: have you ever been tempted to say, 'Right, to hell with that. I'm finished. I'm off. That's it. That's final. That's no more'?

NIVEN: No. *Death*, immediate death, that is, I think. I mean look, even a man who has worked all his life in—in a bank or in a coal mine or anything. They're miserable when they stop. *I'd* be miserable . . . I mean, I'd do one picture a year. I'd do my lectures and I'd write my nonsense and I'd do some television—keep busy. Spend much more time with the family.

RUSSELL: The book must have made you an enormous amount of money. Has it? Has it?

NIVEN: Well, I suppose it will make a nice chunk, you know. It's unbelievably lucky, let's face it, . . . fantastic bit of luck. And I must say this—that I've made eighty-seven movies and I've got more of a charge out of the success of this book—even if it hadn't made a penny—than out of all eighty-seven put together. It's been the greatest ego polisher of all time. But I'd like to write another one, and I don't see how I can really.

RUSSELL: It's effortless to read, and in the very best sense of the word. And I hope you don't think this is impudent, which it is not meant to be—it's a very good lavatory book, it's a very good book to have by you . . .

(*audience laughter*)

. . . do you know what I mean? I mean you can leap in and out of it. And it doesn't tax you in any kind of way. Was it a great effort to write?

NIVEN: Well I tell you, it was and it wasn't, because when I started to write it and I sent it off to a friend of mine—to Hamish Hamilton the publisher, he immediately wanted me to go on. He immediately bought it in fact when I'd only written one chapter. And then I had to work. I tried terribly hard to write well, and oddly enough I remembered things I was taught about writing English at school— trying not to say 'The man was mahogany coloured through the sun' —you know, all those clichés—and trying to say something else, and trying not to split infinitives. I tried to do the rudimentary part of writing it better. I did work hard on it. I only worked when it was raining, I didn't work too hard. But I've had a huge advance from Putnams, the American publisher, for the next one, and I've spent it! (*audience laughter*)

RUSSELL: At the end of the book one thing extraordinary occurred to me which is that your life, and your early life particularly, was spent on a high plane of what we would now regard as permissiveness, and yet your last chapter in the book is quite a sharp attack against present-day permissiveness by young people—by the present-day young people. Are you objecting strongly to one specific incident or are you not in tune with present-day activities of young people?

NIVEN: Well, I think I made rather a mistake there. I've had a lot of back-chat from a lot of young friends. Because I didn't mean to attack, as a matter of fact. I said in the book how difficult it is for actors to get off the stage, and how difficult it was for me to get off at the end of the book—to finish it, and I just thought up this way of finishing it. I described a party I went to—a 'pot' party, you know. Everything was going on. I was taken there by one of my god-daughters. I've got eighteen god-daughters, so nobody knows which one it was. And I described it faithfully, I really think. I didn't mean to knock it that much. I didn't enjoy it, but then also, looking you right in the eye and all your millions of listeners, when Errol Flynn and I shared a house together—I hate to say that was a quarter of a century ago or more—Errol went to Africa on a film and he came back with some stuff called kief which we used to cut up and put into cigarettes and smoke, and it was fine. We did it for weeks. Marihuana —same thing. So there's nothing new to me about that. I happened to give it up very soon after that. And I didn't mean to knock it. I think that the young generation is great, as a matter of fact. I hated that party and I hated the films they were showing—pure pornography. I hated that. I'm not against permissiveness a bit, I think that our whole hope is the youth anyway of this country, of every country. I'm *terribly* against violence. I'm not against pornography, honestly. If it's shown to children, I'm a hundred thousand per cent against it. If grown-ups really want to go and see a dirty picture on a Saturday afternoon, then why not make it a nice clean little movie house and let them go and see a dirty picture? I don't see that that's the end of the world at all. But violence – if you can see on television twenty-five times a night a way to knock off a policeman or rob a bank, sooner or later some moron's going to do it. This is the real danger to me.

RUSSELL: Are you a coward?

NIVEN: Oh yes – yes I am. I mean I went through the war for six-and-a-half years but I was scared out of my bloody wits.

(*audience laughter*)

And I think everybody was, really.

RUSSELL: Well now, look, we've been talking a lot about time – about looking back over all these years. You still remain slim and elegant. Do you diet?

NIVEN: No. I've – em – knocked off the hard booze. Errol Flynn did that for me, he took my quota. We had a house called 'Cirrhosis by the Sea' at one point.

(*audience laughter*)

RUSSELL: I have to draw this conversation to a close. It's been very enjoyable. Before you go, we got through the entire part of this evening without mentioning the title of your book: *The Moon's a Balloon*. There are at large in this world, nine hundred and ninety-nine thousand, nine hundred and ninety-nine copies of that book. You may or may not believe this. I know there aren't more because, I can now reveal to you, I have here the one millionth copy, which is a specially prepared and beautiful copy, bound in leather, tooled and everything. It's an enormous privilege, enormous pleasure to open it, and to deliver it with all our congratulations into your hands, David Niven.

NIVEN: Oh, that is marvellous. Thank you very much. Thank you.

(*applause*)

RUSSELL: So you can take it home to the South of France, put it on your shelves and dust it.

NIVEN: I'm very grateful. I'm very touched and I'm very grateful. Thank you very much.

RUSSELL: And I hope it reminds you in some small way of the pleasure that you have given to us all tonight. David Niven.

(*applause*)

EDNA O'BRIEN

RUSSELL: I'm particularly delighted to welcome my next guest, because she didn't really want to come on the show at all.

When I first invited her along, she claimed her diary was full of other engagements, and it was only when she decided to push them all on one side that she admitted that the real reason had been that she just hated so-called chat-shows.

And so, ladies and gentlemen, flattered I am to welcome Miss Edna O'Brien.

(*music; applause*)

EDNA O'BRIEN: It's strange that you should say that. I didn't want to come on. It wasn't that my diary was full — my diary is always, and quite rightly, empty. It was another reason — apart from nervousness. Reluctance, shall we say. Coming here in the car which you sent for me, we went very astray. We were in EC4 and EC3 — which aren't near each other, I might add . . . and I thought, 'Ah! Rescue! I'll never get there'. And then I remembered that Karl Gustav Jung, my great dead father-figure, said he tried to go to Rome three times, but the first time a storm prevented it; the second time, I think it was a human relationship; and the third time he fainted in the ticket office.

(*audience laughter*)

Anyhow, he said that he felt the spirit of Rome wasn't ready for him.

(*audience laughter*)

RUSSELL: Have you decided anything about my spirit? Am I about ready for it?

EDNA O'BRIEN: For Rome?

RUSSELL: No, for you.

EDNA O'BRIEN: Let's stay in Rome. It's safer. I spent this summer there. It's insane. Motor-cyclists going through the brain. I found the heat intolerable. Everyone talked a lot — even more than I talk, and that's saying a lot. And one day I was very hot in Rome and I had a mirage and found myself writing — forgive me for discussing writing —

> *The birds flew, I thought they were kites —*
> *The birds sang, I thought they were murmurs —*
> *The birds scattered, I thought they were bullets.*
> *The birds were many things on that crazy day.*
> *But in the evening they were birds again,*
> *And my heart stood still.*

And Rome was exquisite for about twenty minutes — in the evening. Now to come back to you: I think you are ready for my spirit — being as I'm here.

RUSSELL: Now, for somebody who talks so beautifully, which you do, I'm surprised that you devote endless hours to writing — which is a lonely occupation — when talking is such a convivial, gregarious operation.

EDNA O'BRIEN: Yes, but it's not from where one is centred, you see. I have heard, and I believe it to be true, that Irish people are very split between that kind of story-telling thing, like the bard who went from town to town, usually blind — from drink, no doubt — between that and actually sitting down and writing it. I find I prefer to write than to talk. The odd night, sitting up late, the embers and all that, is nice for talking, but writing is, despite the fact that one can hardly ever do it, a kind of baptism of the self. It's a sort of elevation.

RUSSELL: Do you talk to yourself at all?

EDNA O'BRIEN: Constantly! — You know, about keys and how to put the key in the door and is the gas on or off — gibberish . . .

(*audience laughter*)

RUSSELL: Now, you brought up the question of Irishness on your own. I was surprised and relieved that despite your perambulations through EC3 and EC4 that you were in fact here on time. I mean, the fact that you arrived here on time is slightly un-Irish.

EDNA O'BRIEN: Well, Irish women — let us say it and underline it — are a different kettle of fish to Irish men.

RUSSELL: Really?

EDNA O'BRIEN: Oh yes. Irish women are very good mothers — wonderful nurses — as this whole country must know . . .

(*applause*)

. . . and are staunchly reliable. I think I am very reliable. Irish men are — something else which I don't think we need to go into.

(*audience laughter*)

RUSSELL: I can't even push you slightly towards that cliff, can I? No?

EDNA O'BRIEN: Not me.

RUSSELL: Lips are sealed.

EDNA O'BRIEN: Good soldiers, shall we say?

RUSSELL: What kind of mum and dad did you have?

EDNA O'BRIEN: I vary in how I react to them by the minute. I think if one — as I must have wanted to do — if one wanted to write works of fiction, they were a most fertile feeding ground. I think they were in many ways killers, but they did give birth to me. So I feel mixed about it. And of course what I forgot when I was young and what I keep forgetting in my sometimes rage, I keep forgetting they were the result of where they came from. It's a very religious and very strangling kind of place.

At the moment I am writing a book called *Love*. But love of course includes also 'hate' and 'marry' and 'adore' and all the other sorts of tributaries to it. They feature in it thus:

> *Should I write and tell them that I hate them, these parents on the very verge of their extreme unctions. Should I tell them why I hate them? Because I know why. I hate him because he murdered me in each and all of my tiniest inclinations, so that I walked with a stoop, thought with a dread, and spoke the utmost, untruthful, placating drivel. And she — she stitched me back on; she got a big packing needle — that was her heart — and a big bale of coarse twine — that was her will — and whenever I walked abroad and felt the air, or met with the spirit of nature, she called me back, 'Quick! Quick!', to the world of stirabout and bowel movements, to the cold dark rooms, reeking of vomited drink, to the cold dark rooms, waiting for the next hideous commission of sin.*

But I have some pleasant memories too, and I fully recognise my own propensity for untruth. For instance, I found a love letter which I wrote years ago, and it began, 'My darling . . .' and I couldn't remember which darling it had been addressed to.

(*applause*)

RUSSELL: You make the air around you very still — everybody went very quiet. I suspect a lot of people find it attractive. Do men find your stillness attractive?

EDNA O'BRIEN: I doubt it. I haven't been told so. I think that very, very nervous people who burrow in their central nervous systems are, as a kind of defence, over-quiet. I'd like to be still . . . I mean, look at other people, and look at statues and figures, and flowers and all things, and not speak. I like emanations. When I hear myself talking, I think, 'Ah, somebody has put the unfortunate sixpence in the slot — my voice box.'

But I love two kinds of ways to be and for other people to be too. I love enormous, zany, energetic aliveness, and complete repose. I once thought I would like to live my life in sections, a monastery for a period and then a wild kind of—what Janis Joplin used to call a 'night on the town' life, and then some real work. But I couldn't decide if the work should come after the monastery or if the living should.

(*Russell laughs*)

Yes, I think the work would be best after the living.

RUSSELL: Now, in some of the stories you have written—I am thinking particularly of *The Love Object*—you have described what it is like to be in love and to fall out of love—not to fall out of it, but to come through.

EDNA O'BRIEN: *It* falls out of one—like lights, animal lights.

RUSSELL: In many ways, *The Love Object* is a kind of handbook for people who are in that kind of situation. I found it very interesting, but there were certain tips and guide lines which I was picking up from that experience which would obviously be useful. Do people write to you a lot for advice?

EDNA O'BRIEN: I get some letters, seldom for advice, because that's too blatant. But when people write to me they very often write and say quite lovely things as well as quite . . . suggestive things, and sometimes wicked—I mean cursing. But I feel that my return imprecations are quite strong.

But *The Love Object* was an autopsy on a love affair written at a time when I wouldn't have survived if I hadn't set it all down, and mercilessly.

It sounds very cruel, but I don't mean it cruelly, and I didn't when I wrote it. I was trying to, perhaps for myself, just look at why I had been so bound over. You know, I wanted—and may not have succeeded—I wanted to try and ask myself what this whole obsession was. Was it to do with sex? Was it to do with religion? Was it to do with one's parents? Was it to do with oneself? Was it to do with the unfortunate man? Was it to do with hoping it would never end, or hoping it would end at once? And I have something very distressing to tell you: I wrote that several years ago, and I find myself almost in an identical position today, having learnt nothing, or very little.

RUSSELL: But that's a cheerful thing to say, isn't it? That's a reasonably joyful thing to say, because it has conceded optimism. Maybe there aren't odd things you can learn about ultimate truths in life.

EDNA O'BRIEN: I can see the stupidity in it, and the repetition.

RUSSELL: But do you know what I mean? Maybe there *aren't* ultimate things to learn. Maybe if we ever learn the final thing which we are supposed to learn, that's the end of our life. And as long as we are open to these kinds of repressions and hurts and pains and joys, we are continuing to live.

EDNA O'BRIEN: Ah yes, that's true, except that I think it would be preferable to be in love with a lot of people.

RUSSELL: All at once?

EDNA O'BRIEN: If that sounds like advocating promiscuity — grand! I'm for it. But you load down one poor man or woman or child or something with this great legacy of love, whereas if it could be just — you know, like dancing — step here, step there — I'd like that. I'd like that because it would — it would take the — I was about to say it would take the darkness out of it, but I like the darkness. It makes poems.

RUSSELL: Have you ever tried to commit suicide?

EDNA O'BRIEN: I never have actually, so to speak, got the razor blades out. I have thought about it and I have thought about the fact that within a certain hour — that that might be the only resort. I once met somebody from Amsterdam who told me he was going to have a shop — a supermarket, a suicide supermarket where you went in as if you were going to buy your dinner, and at the end of it, you went to your suicide. I had thought that if that existed (and I don't advocate it), I might have been tempted. But it's silly, because afterwards, a day later, one would say, 'Why? Why?'

Have you ever tried to commit suicide?

RUSSELL: No, I haven't. — And I'm even less inclined now.

EDNA O'BRIEN: It's strange that you should ask me. I have often looked at your programme . . .

(*audience outburst*)

RUSSELL: The last thing to say to you is, one of the things I find very cheerful about you is your extreme and extraordinary love of your two kids, who are obviously a great support in your life.

EDNA O'BRIEN: Yes, I love numerous children, but I particularly love my own children, because I have had access to them, and they to me, for a long time. They are very direct. Children do not accede to you, and yet you kind of know they like to be in your area. It is so easy to be sentimental about children. But I love what they do for me, which is to allow me at last to be myself. Children don't bring up false notes. They sometimes bring up — you know — irritating ones. I remember once when my eldest son was little, he took some pebbles and put them all the way up his nose, thinking they would come down . . .

(*audience laughter*)

. . . and they didn't, and that wasn't so funny . . . I'm a very bad doctor: I was taking a thorn out of his — it must have been his right hand — the other day, otherwise he could have taken it out himself — he's a big lad now — and he said, 'God, mother, you're shaking,' he said, 'God, you're a coward.' I said, 'Yes, I am a coward.'

RUSSELL: Well, you are one of the nicest cowards I have met for a long time, and thank you for making the air still and the night enchanting, Edna O'Brien.

EDNA O'BRIEN: Thank you all, very much.

(*applause*)

BARRY HUMPHRIES
(ALIAS EDNA EVERAGE)

RUSSELL: Welcome back to England, Barry Humphries.

(*applause; music*)

HUMPHRIES: (*enters dressed as middle-aged woman*) How do you do, Simon. I'm terribly sorry, but Barry couldn't be here.

RUSSELL: No, Russell's my name. Russell Harty.

HUMPHRIES: Russell. I'm so sorry. How do you do, dear? You've done wonderfully well, haven't you? Wonderfully well.

RUSSELL: I'm a bit taken aback.

HUMPHRIES: You started with nothing, and look at you now. How do you do, dear? I'm awfully sorry but Barry Humphries couldn't be here this evening. We've just flown in from Australia and we're both suffering from 'jet-lag', I'm afraid.

RUSSELL: How is it showing itself, your suffering from . . .?

HUMPHRIES: Well, I'm feeling very, very well, but Barry isn't terribly well, poor pet. He's back in the hotel and of course, he has just had a vasectomy . . .

(*audience laughter*)

. . . on his Diner's Card.

(*audience laughter*)

He's not a hundred per cent, so he said, 'Edna, would you just pop along?' How do you do? My name is Edna Everage, housewife superstar.

RUSSELL: Are you happy to be back in England?

HUMPHRIES: I'm thrilled to bits, Simon. It's gorgeous to be here. I think it's a lovely city. I've always had a very, very soft spot in my heart for the Old Country.

RUSSELL: How long is it since you were here last?

HUMPHRIES: It's *far* too long, it is really. Goodness me, I think it — well, of course you were . . . not a very well known little person when I left.

RUSSELL: I was a very unknown big person . . .

HUMPHRIES: Not very well known, but you've done, as I say,

41

wonderfully. And I think the marvellous thing about it is, dear – if I may say so – that you're open to suggestion . . .

(*audience laughter*)

I think in a position like yours you have to be, you know, to ask little questions, and you have to satisfy – if I may say so – a ceaseless intellectual curiosity. That's something that you do, and I think that'll help you to the top. You've got a long climb but I think you'll make it.

RUSSELL: There should be wild applause at this moment, shouldn't there? But it's absolutely quiet.

HUMPHRIES: You've got a lovely little studio audience here too. I hope you don't mind my coming here.

RUSSELL: No, I'm – I'm . . .

HUMPHRIES: I nearly rang up and said that Barry couldn't be here, but I think he'll be watching from his sick-bed.

RUSSELL: I'm delighted to have you – and I'm a little astounded by your appearance, if you'll forgive me for saying that. I mean, everything seems to match. Did you go on a ceaseless, intellectual quest to make everything match?

HUMPHRIES: Well, I see from the little monitor that we have colour television. I think you're wonderful, you English people.

(*audience laughter*)

You've got so little, but you've got colour television. I think it's one of the main things, particularly for the sick and the invalids and the older folk. I think it's marvellous. We haven't got it yet in Australia. We have four channels.

RUSSELL: You do?

HUMPHRIES: Yes, we do.

RUSSELL: What are they called: 1, 2, 3, 4?

HUMPHRIES: I don't remember, dear. It seems like a dream – all that travelling. But I have teamed – for those of you who haven't got colour television – I have teamed a mustard sheath, with mango gloves, and a very large houndstooth coat. I bought this in London, as a matter of fact, on my last trip. And I have those very practical, white lace-up vinyl shoes, and they're marvellous for just trudging around London. I enjoy it, I think it's a pip of a place, I really do. I think people – in Australia we feel so sorry for England, but I think it's mistaken . . .

RUSSELL: Why? Why do you feel sorry for us?

HUMPHRIES: I do – I think a lot of people are patronising about it.

RUSSELL: Wait a minute, who's patronising about what? Are we patronising about Australia, or are you . . .?

HUMPHRIES: A lot of people in Australia — can I just talk to you before the programme starts, just quietly, dear?

RUSSELL: Yes, yes. Just you alone.

HUMPHRIES: A lot of people in Australia, who feel — you know, just because none of you can afford meat any more, and that kind of thing . . . I brought some food parcels over by the way. I brought some dripping.

RUSSELL: Dripping?

HUMPHRIES: My home in Melbourne during the hostilities was a 'Fat for Britain' depot. All the neighbours used to deposit their old dripping on my front doorstep. We used to whisk it up to the Old Country. I used to send coconut ice over here, too. As a matter of fact, I'm going to look up the little family that we sent it to, I am.

RUSSELL: Really?

HUMPHRIES: But, where was I, dear? Oh yes, a lot of people are talking about turning Australia into a republic, and abolishing 'God Save the Queen' and that kind of thing. But I'd like you to know that the majority of feeling for the Old Country in Australia is one of . . . deep loyalty and profound sympathy.

RUSSELL: For whom?

HUMPHRIES: Well, I mean, I just think that — you've got little problems, and I think that perhaps if Australia did detach itself from the Commonwealth, just as an experiment, it would give you just a little rest, you English people, because it takes you all your time to look after the Portuguese, doesn't it?

RUSSELL: Do we — do we *own* the Portuguese?

HUMPHRIES: I don't think so, but I think they're very dependent on you. I don't know — I'm just a silly woman, and a housewife.

RUSSELL: Well, now, wait a minute . . .

HUMPHRIES: I've had a wonderful success, by the way.

RUSSELL: You've had a wonderful success?

HUMPHRIES: Oh yes, I've been in a motion picture recently.

RUSSELL: Really? — Who spotted you?

HUMPHRIES: Well, Mr Barry Humphries.

RUSSELL: Really?

HUMPHRIES: That's why I'm over here. He's a wonderful little person, he's terribly, terribly talented.

RUSSELL: Is he a relative of yours?

HUMPHRIES: That's probably why he had the vasectomy . . . Beg your pardon, dear?

(*audience laughter*)

He's no relative of mine at all. He's very, very well known. I'd say he's world-famous in Melbourne.

RUSSELL: Right.

HUMPHRIES: And he spotted me. As a matter of fact, do you know where he *did* spot me? I come from a Melbourne suburb called Moonee Ponds, and he spotted me in a Passion Play at Holy Trinity Church, Mozart Avenue, Moonee Ponds. I was playing Mary Magdalene.

RUSSELL: You were?

HUMPHRIES: Yes, I was.

RUSSELL: What were you wearing?

HUMPHRIES: Oh, I was wearing a . . . a sheath.

RUSSELL: Is that all?

HUMPHRIES: Not a *mustard* sheath. I was wearing a white sheath, and it had some red trimmings on it. I thought of auditioning for *Jesus Christ, Superstar* as a matter of fact, but I thought I'd leave it to young people like yourself who've got such a long struggle before them. He spotted me, and he said that I had a potential, and so he asked me to help him in some of his wonderful shows, and I've been over here with him before. Some of the older listeners or the invalids might remember that I have made appearances on television before, over here.

RUSSELL: This is not your first taste . . . ?

HUMPHRIES: I've got a lot of confidence, Simon.

RUSSELL: Yes . . .

HUMPHRIES: So that's helped me a lot in my life. Lots of confidence, because I think that it is important. It's half the battle, isn't it? That, and listening to suggestions.

RUSSELL: That's my cue to make a suggestion to you, isn't it?

HUMPHRIES: Well, not really, dear.

RUSSELL: Well, what I'm going to suggest is – he spotted you in Moonee Ponds Passion Play?

HUMPHRIES: Oh yes. And then . . .

RUSSELL: But what did he offer you at that time?

HUMPHRIES: Well, he asked me if I would first help him with the dressing: his quick changes, and that kind of thing, because he does different characters. And I was very, very interested. He was so clever. It was a new world opening up for me. I mean wonderful, wonderful people. And then he told me to come over to the Old Country with him, and we made this film about my nephew's life story. I have a nephew called Barry MacKenzie, from the Sydney side of the family. That side of the family's always been a little bit C-O-M-M-O-N, Simon. A little bit O-R-D-I-N-A-R-Y . . .

(*audience laughter*)

Sydney people *are*, they're a little bit – they don't have the refinement of Melbourne folk. But anyway, they made this wonderful film, and it's been playing in Australia to packed houses, and it's going to come to England. Won't that be a thrill?

RUSSELL: That'll be an enormous thrill.

HUMPHRIES: I'm in it.

RUSSELL: What part do you play in it?

HUMPHRIES: I play myself, and I also feel that I'm a moral custodian of Australia, in the film.

RUSSELL: You don't carry a spear or a shield . . .?

HUMPHRIES: No, I carry a handbag as a matter of fact . . . And of course my sheath. But the thing is –

RUSSELL (*laughing*): Wait a minute, wait a minute. Hold on before you rocket away. Why do you have to *erect* yourself . . . as a moral custodian – as a moral custodian of Australia?

HUMPHRIES: Was that *al*together necessary, dear?

RUSSELL: As the moral custodian of Australia! Is it in need of moral custody?

HUMPHRIES: Well, no. I just think that – you see, there's these sex films that are coming out now. I haven't seen them – I have to be frank there, I haven't seen them. I don't think it is necessary to see them. I know what they're about.

(*audience laughter*)

I'm a married woman (*audience laughter*) – I have three wonderful, wonderful kiddies: Brucie, Valmae and Kenny. Wonderful, wonderful kiddies, and . . .

RUSSELL: Do they work, or do they play?

HUMPHRIES: Well – no. My son Brucie is married to a lovely lass, Joyleen. She's a Sydney girl and he's a Melbourne boy. I warned him about mixed marriages, but he takes no notice. And then, my daughter, Valmae and my little son – my little son, Kenny – is still looking for Miss Right. He is, yes. He looks in some rather peculiar places from time to time. He's still looking, and he believes in happiness, he does. He's a member of the Gay Liberation in Melbourne. His little friends – look, if I've bought myself a new frock or a new pair of shoes, or a little new hat or something of that kind, on one of my trips, and I look in my wardrobe and I can't find it, I know where

45

to go. I do. He dresses up. I think he's going to be in the theatre, d'you know that?

(*audience laughter*)

I think he's probably going to follow in your profession.

RUSSELL: Really!

HUMPHRIES: It's possible.

RUSSELL: Well, what does your little girl do?

HUMPHRIES: Oh—oh, Valmae, she's married and got a wonderful family: Karen, Lee and little Craig.

RUSSELL: And where do they live?

HUMPHRIES: They live in Melbourne.

RUSSELL: What kind of a house do they have?

HUMPHRIES: Cream brick veneer. That's one of the things that shocks Australians when they come to England. All the homes are close together. It's so sad for you.

RUSSELL: Sad it may be, but it's the way we have to live and where we have to work.

HUMPHRIES: Of course it is, of course it is. 'Live and let live' is what I say. I've always said it.

RUSSELL: Right. And you're right indeed. Can I make another suggestion?

HUMPHRIES: Certainly.

RUSSELL: Or *may* I make another suggestion?

HUMPHRIES (*lovingly*): What a sweet and natural person you are!

RUSSELL: I'm following your lead. Has our Old Country changed since you saw us last?

HUMPHRIES: Well, look—as I say, I've only just really stepped off the wonderful Qantas jet. I haven't noticed a great deal of difference. There were still some white people left . . .

(*audience laughter and applause*)

RUSSELL: Now, wait a minute—you stepped off the Qantas . . .

HUMPHRIES: Have I noticed any changes?

RUSSELL: Right.

HUMPHRIES: Well, the people are naturally a little bit thinner. They are hungry all the time, poor things. That's why I've brought a plentiful supply of dripping.

(*audience laughter*)

Otherwise, I think they're pulling down too many buildings. May I strike a more serious note just for a moment?

RUSSELL: Go right ahead . . .

HUMPHRIES: I think that we Australians, we come here as tourists, in

46

search of our heritage, and I think it's such a pity that so much of it is coming down. I think that somehow, when you look at the wonderful works of Christopher Wren and Michelangelo, it seems such a shame that some of these newer buildings don't have the same feeling about them. Don't you agree? I feel that. However, I've taken a lot of slides all the same.

RUSSELL: You have?

HUMPHRIES: Yes.

RUSSELL: With your Kodak Instamatic?

HUMPHRIES: Yes, I'm quite a cunning one with my aperture (*laughs*) . . .

(*audience laughter*)

RUSSELL: Now your relatives, or your family, have a trick or a habit, from time to time, of getting into more trouble than is good for them They are a bit accident prone.

HUMPHRIES: The Sydney side of my family, the MacKenzie side, they're quite naughty.

RUSSELL: I mean—a lot of naughty things happen to them, don't they? Or they make naughty things happen?

HUMPHRIES: They do. They don't quite behave themselves as they might. As a matter of fact, when we were coming over to make the film of *Barry MacKenzie*, I was travelling with my nephew, Barry, in the plane. Now, he must have been hungry or something, because he had a very large tin of mixed vegetable salad . . . I won't mention the brand, because it might make you ill. Anyway, he opened the tin of mixed vegetable salad, and because it was probably a little bit cumbersome he was looking for some way of eating it. We were travelling tourist, I'm afraid—'economy', as it's called. And, he emptied the mixed vegetable salad into one of those Qantas airsickness bags, and he was nibbling away at it—and of course some of it got on his little fingers, and on his double-breasted navy blue pin-stripe, and on his old Melbourne grey tie, and he was naturally licking the potato salad off his fingers, and eating out of the bag, and the poor little Qantas hostess—her name was Janice if I remember correctly. (All Qantas hostesses are called Janice.) You know—the poor little thing had a technicolour yawn in First Class.

(*audience laughter*)

RUSSELL: A what?

HUMPHRIES: A technicolour yawn.

RUSSELL: What's that?

HUMPHRIES: A little tummy upset. I don't normally use that phraseology. A liquid laugh. Sometimes known as parking a tiger. I only know this because my nephew is a naughty boy, and he uses this horrible Sydney language, and some of it has rubbed off . . . a nasty stain on his character, if you ask me.

RUSSELL: Now, finally, if I may bring us to the brink of the conversation, which is that we are all quite upset about the forward-looking attitude of Gough Whitlam, your Prime Minister. I mean he's trying to sever us — you from me — and you from us and everything. We don't really want to lose you, but if you're going to be independent-minded, we have to make other arrangements. Because you're making other arrangements, aren't you? I mean, you're making your own National Anthem.

HUMPHRIES: We're going to leave you Portugal.

(*audience laughter*)

No. No. I feel very strongly about England. I do. I think that Australians are sometimes too brutal about England. After all, it still is a member of the Commonwealth.

(*audience laughter*)

The thing is, I'm not a political woman — I don't get myself mixed up in that sort of thing. Life is too short. I haven't met Gough Whitlam. I have met his wife. She is very, very statuesque, to put it mildly . . . I'm not a Labour supporter. I'm sorry. But I think it would be a pity if we lost track of England altogether. I would point this out — that the Queen and her doings, and the Royal Family are always on the front page of our newspapers . . . And we had Lord Snowdon and Princess Margaret in Western Australia very, very recently, and she was so radiant and wonderful. She reached many, many hearts and we'll always feel that.

RUSSELL: I'm sure that nothing has been so radiant, or reached so many hearts tonight as you, Mrs Edna Everage.

HUMPHRIES (*getting up to go*): We always feel that . . .

RUSSELL: Now, wait a minute . . .

HUMPHRIES: I think I will *have* to go, if I may. I'd love to go on chatting to you, but they gave me lots and lots of cups of tea before I went on this programme, and I'm afraid I'll have to excuse myself.

RUSSELL: . . . and duty calls you.

HUMPHRIES: I have to aim Alice at the Armitage!

(*audience laughter*)

Goodbye, dear.

(*applause*)

APRIL ASHLEY

RUSSELL: Now my next guest is someone whose name has been the target of many a ripe remark over the past ten years. She first came to public notice when her name was blazoned across the front pages of the Sunday newspapers as the man who had had the affrontery to undergo an operation to become a woman. Since then, she has undergone the even more painful business of divorcing the man she married, and being told by a judge that she didn't measure up to being a woman anyway. Well, she's here to tell us where she stands tonight. Ladies and gentlemen, Miss April Ashley.

(music; applause)

Now, could you ease yourself into there? (April sits down next to Russell.) It's a very medieval gown, that, isn't it?

APRIL: No, I think it's Japanese actually. It's made in England by a Japanese.

RUSSELL: Right. Now let's get on to you, how many years ago now is it since you had your operation?

APRIL: My God, I can't remember. I think in the 1950s.

RUSSELL: Well, when you decided to do that, was your Mum alive?

APRIL: My mother is still alive, I think . . .

RUSSELL: At the last count, that is? What was her reaction to your decision to have the operation?

APRIL: She thought I had had a nose job.

(audience laughter)

RUSSELL: Well . . .! You told her, though, that you were going to do it—before you actually had the operation?

APRIL: No.

RUSSELL: Well, how did you describe it?

APRIL: Well I thought it was a very private thing, a thing like this. Why burden other people with those problems? I mean, I'm not going to say to my Ma, you know, 'Gosh I'm going to have this major operation.' I think it's incredibly private to have any kind of operation, in fact.

RUSSELL: And that one oughtn't to talk about it?

APRIL: No, I think when you've had it done you suddenly say 'Help!' You know, 'Look, I need a bit of cheering up and I need you to look pretty. Come and see me.'

RUSSELL: When you had the change, you then got married, didn't you, and after that got divorced?

APRIL: Divorced after seven years of being known as Mrs Corbett, which was quite a shock.

RUSSELL: To whom?

APRIL: To me. For seven years I'd been plain Mrs Corbett – well, not *plain*: I was the Honourable Mrs Corbett.

(*audience laughter*)

RUSSELL: You went right to the heights, baby, didn't you?

APRIL: Absolutely!

RUSSELL: Right up.

APRIL: But I was known as Mrs Corbett, I worked as Mrs Corbett, my insurance card was Mrs Corbett . . . all those boring things, you know.

RUSSELL: Did that help you to condition yourself to your new state?

APRIL: I didn't need any help.

RUSSELL: You didn't?

APRIL (*pointing to her brain*): You never change here, your sex.

RUSSELL: And you decided at a very early age up there that you were female?

APRIL: Well, *I* didn't decide. I don't know who decides those things, but *I* certainly didn't.

RUSSELL: God, or a god, decided that . . .

APRIL: *A* god, let's put it like that.

RUSSELL: Or your genes, or your conditioning . . .

APRIL: Well, yes. It's so difficult to talk about it because you grow up, and there you are, you're an ugly child, or a beautiful child. As it happened, I was a rather ugly child . . .

RUSSELL: An ugly boy?

APRIL: . . . and suddenly . . .

RUSSELL: Now wait a minute, you were an ugly boy . . . ?

APRIL: No, no, no, we are talking about babies, first of all. And then, instead of developing like a boy, you suddenly find hips, and you suddenly find breasts arriving, it's terrifying, absolutely terrifying because you know that one thing should be happening and another thing is in fact happening.

RUSSELL: Are you still an object of curiosity in England?

50

APRIL: Oh, I think so. Why do you think they are all staring so intently?

(*audience laughter*)

RUSSELL: Well, a lot of them may be surprised that you are so beautiful to look at.

APRIL: Yes, and I must point out to them that I've not done anything like *Whicker's World* . . .

(*audience laughter*)

Nothing, but nothing, has been touched on my face. My nose is my own — my mother's ignorance has nothing to do with my nose.

RUSSELL: Whatever else may not be . . .

APRIL: Everything else is natural. And you know, this is something else which absolutely *kills* me, they talk about a female trapped in a male's body (*turning to the audience*). Well, I think if I went home to bed with a few of these people and stripped off, they'd be quite amazed . . .

(*audience laughter*)

. . . because there is certainly nothing male about my body.

RUSSELL: Really? Does that mean you can enjoy absolutely normal sex relations with a man?

APRIL: Yes . . . if I can give you one tiny incident from the court case — biologically, I'm a male, but socially I'm a female. Now, if a man knows that I am biologically a male and goes to bed with me, he is a homosexual. But what happens to the poor man — and I've done it — who goes to bed with me as a female and doesn't know the darndest thing about it? He thinks he's made a big score, you know, and he thinks, 'Christ, look at her. She's gorgeous!'

RUSSELL: Well, he may not be awfully used to going to bed with women . . . if you see what I mean.

APRIL: Well, I don't think I like virgin men.

RUSSELL: Do you believe that a man has to be a man and a woman has to be a woman, and there is not an area between those two in which the two may overlap?

APRIL: Well, Russell, I would love you to meet a man called Dr Armstrong. He would show you so many deviations in the sexual lives of . . .

RUSSELL: You see, the word 'deviation' is a kind of loaded word . . .

APRIL: Yes, but he's invented something called the Sexual Rainbow, and my God! there is every colour of the rainbow in that rainbow.

RUSSELL: And those are *natural* colours you're talking about?

APRIL: Yes, and it doesn't mean that every man has a little bit of

51

femininity in him, and every woman has masculinity in her. You see, it's like meeting somebody. Every time you meet somebody they bring out something different in you.

RUSSELL: Right.

APRIL: At my age, I'm never surprised at what was brought out in me. I've never found a woman to bring out the lesbian in me yet . . . Should we use that word, by the way . . .?

RUSSELL: Well, it's too late. It's used now.

(*audience uproar*)

APRIL: But I mean, come the day that it might happen, I wouldn't say, 'Definitely not'.

RUSSELL: You wouldn't close your eyes to *any* experience, in fact?

APRIL: Well, I think I'd be a fool to close my eyes to anything.

RUSSELL: How old are you?

APRIL (*after long pause*): Thirty-eight and a half.

RUSSELL: Between thirty and forty, in fact?

APRIL: Getting close to forty, hence the lovely grey hairs.

RUSSELL: Right. You are beautifully groomed. Your dress is beautiful, and your face – do you take a lot of time over your make-up?

APRIL: Well, I used to take a very short time, but last year I broke both my wrists.

RUSSELL: How?

APRIL: I fell down the stairs at a certain nightclub in London.

RUSSELL: That's very mundane, I thought you were ski-ing, or falling out of an aeroplane or something.

APRIL: I wouldn't do anything as mundane as ski-ing, by the way. I'd prefer to fall downstairs. No, I broke both my wrists, and this one's deformed permanently now, and making-up takes longer: it takes about an hour and a half.

RUSSELL: Every day?

APRIL: Every day. You see, I work every day at my restaurant and my customers buy my glamour . . .

RUSSELL: So that's part of the deal, in fact?

APRIL: Yes, but they have a lot of fun too.

RUSSELL: How do you view the prospect of old age, from where you are now?

APRIL: Well . . . I long for my autumn years.

RUSSELL: This is where the music ought to start . . .

APRIL: The violins . . .

RUSSELL: Little leaves drifting . . .

APRIL: I long to get away from that April Ashley image. I long not

52

to see any more Press where they say 'Ex-so-and-so'. I long for the little house in the country . . .

RUSSELL: And thatched roof?

APRIL: No, no, no! God forbid! I'd hate a thatched roof. Think of all the lice running round . . .

(*audience laughter*)

Give me a jolly good – sort of Cotswold stone, something solid.

RUSSELL: And you in a poke bonnet?

APRIL: Oh no, not at all! I'd have my lovely long hair. I mean, I'm always going to be proud of my hair. Why shouldn't I be proud of it when I get old, even if it's white?

RUSSELL: Well look, we're vaguely, give or take a year, the same age. On your eightieth birthday, let's get together.

APRIL: Would you like that? I promise it'll be champagne the whole way.

RUSSELL: Will it?

APRIL: Absolutely.

RUSSELL: Well, the conversation has been like a tonic, so that'll be good. April Ashley, thank you.

(*applause*)

RINGO STARR

RUSSELL: Ladies and gentlemen, that man of many developing talents, Mr Ringo Starr.

(*applause*)

You going to give me a cigarette?

RINGO: Do you want one? I thought you didn't smoke.

RUSSELL: I think it's not good manners, but if you're doing it, I'll try one. Does anybody mind? No, they don't. And a light.

RINGO: That's really great. Down 'ere they're [the audience] all not allowed to smoke and we are.

RUSSELL: Do you know why they're not allowed to smoke? These are the most advanced television studios in the history of the entire world and if you get a lot of smoke whizzing its way up, all the sprinkler valves in the ceiling pour foam over everybody.

RINGO: I thought they worked by heat, not by smoke, those things.

RUSSELL: Well then, let's generate some heat, shall we?

RINGO: Well, we're gettin' far out, Russell, so let's get into it.

RUSSELL: All right. Now, one of the reasons why you're dressed like that, Mr Starr . . .

RINGO: Well, one of the reasons . . . (*stands up slowly*)

RUSSELL: Give them a good look.

(*applause*)

RINGO: . . . is because we're here to plug a new movie, *That'll Be the Day*, which is about teddy-boys, like the 'sixties and late 'fifties. The only way I get new clothes is when I do a film, you know.

(*audience laughter*)

That's why I put 'em on for you.

RUSSELL: Nobody's ever seen you naked, so presumably you're in work all the time.

RINGO: A few people have seen me naked.

RUSSELL: I mean the world hasn't, has it?

RINGO: No, the world hasn't.

RUSSELL: Right. Now, in the film called *That'll Be the Day*, there is a scene during which you pretend that you pull all the birds in a holiday camp, and am I right in saying this is the first time your bum has appeared on British screens?

RINGO: First time. And probably the last.

RUSSELL: You remember how skilful the director was in cutting your face into that scene!

RINGO: Yeah, yeah.

RUSSELL: So we get both ends at once, if you see what I mean.

RINGO: He's just afraid of Mary Whitehouse.

RUSSELL: Who isn't?

RINGO: *I'm* not afraid of Mary Whitehouse.

RUSSELL: You're not? She represents no challenge to you at all?

RINGO: She doesn't represent anything for me.

RUSSELL: Well, let's leave her strictly to one side. The film is a strong evocation of the 'sixties, as you made in your little pre-announcement.

RINGO: It was terrific for me because that's where I was, you know. I was just one of those loony teddy-boys, standing on the corner.

RUSSELL: Did you feed your own information into the film?

RINGO: Yeah.

RUSSELL: Did they ask for advice from you?

RINGO: Well, I wrote three scenes, though Ray Connolly'll never admit it. (He wrote the film.)

RUSSELL: He won't admit much, that gentleman . . .

RINGO: Have you had him on?

RUSSELL: No, he's had *me* on. However, we're not here to talk about him. What tempted you into it?

RINGO: The main reason I did the film is I just dig all that teddy-boy scene, you know. It's so important to my life. I spent ten years as one of those guys. And it's really important. So just to put on the gear again was a good trip.

RUSSELL: You don't feel that that was anachronistic do you?

RINGO: Well, I don't know what it means . . .

(*audience laughter*)

RUSSELL: I mean, you didn't think it was too out of date? Where's your other glove, by the way?

RINGO: Well, I've only got one.

RUSSELL: Where did you get it from?

RINGO: I got it from my good friend, Marc Bolan, who came in the office today. But why I wear it is another story: I've got two kids at home with chicken-pox and don't want to spread it, you see, so you shake hands with the glove. Have you had chicken-pox?

RUSSELL: I think I have, a long time ago.

RINGO: What did you do before the war, Russell?

(*audience laughter; applause*)

RUSSELL: There is no smart reply to that, but now, a bit more about you. Now where are you in your work situation? (I do hate people who say 'What is your work?')

RINGO: What's *your* job? (*laughs*)

What I did last year was produce two films, direct one of them and appear in three. And do a few sessions. So that was a busy year. This year, at this moment, I'm just in the middle of my album, which I'll be leaping off to after this.

RUSSELL: I must say your office is a tremendous hive of activity. I mean, a lot of telephones . . .

RINGO: It is, you see, because there's so many things going on, like all your pals come in to do the deals or business or whatever they want to get into. What I like about it, it's an open house, so people just come in to make phone calls, have a drink or do whatever they like. It's just a nice atmosphere now.

RUSSELL: But it also looked busy and there were important people there.

RINGO: It always looks busy but no one's really doing anything.

(*audience laughter*)

No, they *are* doing something. I mean, a lot of them are doing a lot of heavy deals, you know. The day you came in we were trying to get the record from the film out in America and find the parts. People listen to an album and they think, 'Oh – twenty minutes a side: that's all there is to it!' No one thinks of the three months of making it, the hustling to get all the cover together, for someone to cut the master. I don't *want* them to remember that. But there's a lot goes into it.

RUSSELL: Do you still see your Mum and Dad?

RINGO: Oh, yeah. I saw me Dad . . . last Monday, down here. The last time I was in Liverpool was the Christmas before last. This Christmas all the folks came down here – there's more room.

RUSSELL: When you went home, did you take a sack for Christmas?

RINGO: Yeah. Well, like it is a sad story, folks. I only went home because my mother had pneumonia. And it gets pretty tough at forty-seven.

(*audience laughter*)

I'm sure she's older than that, but she'd like that.

RUSSELL: She behaves like a forty-seven-year-old . . . Now, did you go into directing films because you were in a position money-wise and influence-wise to be able to go in and say: 'I want to direct'? Or did somebody ring you up and say: 'We think you're a guy with good ideas. You'll be a good director'?

RINGO: No. I went into it because I produced the *Born to Boogie* film, with Marc Bolan and T Rex. I wanted to shoot it how I wanted it to be shot, so I directed it, you know. I get a bit browned off with what they're doing with pop music. And I don't want no editor's trip, you know.

RUSSELL: You wanted it straight down the line.

RINGO: If the artist can perform, you should show the *artist*. If he's performing, why show some editor cutting it all up? Madness! Like a cigarette?

RUSSELL: No, I don't want another one. My throat has gone dry.

RINGO: I mean, the money you're making on this, I should think you buy your own.

(*audience laughter; applause*)

The only drag is, you do all this work and then the editor cuts all my good bits out, you know.

RUSSELL: I've just seen an earring as well, why . . . no, it's not an earring, it's a . . .

RINGO: It's a decal.

RUSSELL: A what?

RINGO: A decal.

RUSSELL: How do you spell that?

RINGO: Um . . . transfer.

(*audience laughter*)

RUSSELL: We've been reading in the newspapers about you trying to get the Beatles back together again.

RINGO: Yeah, I read that too, you know.

(*audience laughter*)

RUSSELL: Is fiction stranger than truth?

RINGO: Most times. I mean, if it's straight, right? I'm doing an album. I did it in Los Angeles, because the producer, Richard Perry, lives there. At the time, it just happens John is living in L.A. and George came into L.A. and, you know, I've known those guys a long time. I was working, so they came down and played on the session. That's all there is, you know. There's nothing further than that. It's not like, 'Here they go, they're gonna get together.' It's just that we still like each other, you know, and work for each other.

RUSSELL: Did it work well? That threesome?

RINGO: We did a great couple of tracks, I'll tell you.

RUSSELL: How much preparation did you have to do for it, or did it just happen?

RINGO: Well, nothing, because I saw John on a Wednesday and said 'Have you got any songs?' and Thursday he said: 'Well, I've got a song. Shall we do it?' It wasn't – like, all planned. It just was so good – it just fell into place, you know.

RUSSELL: Well, I hope it's all rather successful. I hope all your ventures in film are successful. I hope that you continue to present yourself to the nation and to the world as beautifully as you have done tonight. Ringo Starr, thank you very much indeed.

(applause)

TENNESSEE WILLIAMS

RUSSELL: Ladies and gentlemen, please welcome the distinguished playwright, Tennessee Williams.

(*applause*)

When did you first realise that you were a magician?

WILLIAMS: I haven't come to that realisation *yet*. Do you think I should? The concluding lines of my last play were 'Magic is a habit' and Michael York says to his sister in the play, 'Yes, magic is the habit of our existence.' I suppose you mean that kind of magic, living in a sort of unreal world.

RUSSELL: You also have to persuade people that the unreality of your world is very reasonable . . .

WILLIAMS: That, that is what you have to do in any kind of creative work. You have to do that.

RUSSELL: But you're a storyteller as well.

WILLIAMS: Oh, I love telling stories. My stories tend to be very long-winded though.

HARTY: Who did you tell stories to when you were a child? Did you tell stories to the kids in the next street?

WILLIAMS: Oh, yes. I was an endless storyteller. In the mountains at East Tennessee – we used to go there for summer vacations – I was always asked to tell a story and I would tell very spooky ones. And finally I would start shaking, you know. Mother tells me I once said, 'I'm sorry, I'm gettin' scared myself,' and couldn't go on.

RUSSELL: You've said at various times that whenever you hear the word 'genius' used about you . . .

WILLIAMS: I feel for my wallet . . .

(*audience laughter*)

. . . because I don't trust the word. Applied to myself I don't accept it.

RUSSELL: Is that from modesty?

WILLIAMS: I think modesty is a false emotion, but I just don't consider myself [a genius] – I know that I work very hard and, it seems to me, that if I succeeded in learning to write any better, it was only through sheer perseverance.

RUSSELL: But, do you use the word 'genius' yourself about other people?

WILLIAMS: I think I have called Muriel Spark a genius. I'm certain that I've called Jane Bowles, the American novelist, a genius. Certainly I've called Michelangelo a genius. Who hasn't? It's not a word that I use lightly.

RUSSELL: Does your fame and your eminence in any sense weigh heavily upon you? Do you feel it as a — heavy responsibility?

WILLIAMS: I tell you — it makes it more difficult to make friends, yes, to be well known now. I live on a little island called Key West, Florida. I know only two or three people who will speak to me. Because they dislike the fact that I'm too well known, you see.

RUSSELL: Why? Are they jealous of you?

WILLIAMS: I don't know why. During the 'sixties I was very obnoxious. I was sick. And that makes people obnoxious, you know. I would just suddenly announce I was going to fall down, and down I'd go like a tenpin — and they got tired of that.

RUSSELL: You mean they got physically tired at having to pick you up all the time?

WILLIAMS: There was a bit of a breakage, you know.

RUSSELL: You broke furniture?

WILLIAMS: Yes. And chairs, and glasses — that sort of thing.

RUSSELL: Are you as neatly dressed in Key West as you are here?

WILLIAMS: Oh, in Key West one wears next to nothing. You know, you're practically streaking the whole time.

(*audience laughter*)

RUSSELL: Has streaking hit Key West?

WILLIAMS: Oh yes. In Key West it was just a way of life for all since the beginning of time, I think.

RUSSELL: Now you are, or you think you are — or maybe you are, one of the richest writers in the world?

WILLIAMS: I think I'm one of the poorest.

RUSSELL: When you were a struggling writer in the early days, were you grateful for prize money and amounts that came your way by surprise?

WILLIAMS: Oh yes. I started writing between twelve and fourteen and I began to get little prizes, you know, like a $10 prize, a $25 prize . . .

RUSSELL: Which made a difference to you?

WILLIAMS: Enormously. The recognition and having a bit of money.

RUSSELL: What did your mother and father make of you?

WILLIAMS: My mother was much more tolerant than my father, actually, but . . .

RUSSELL: Did she love you?

WILLIAMS: (*pauses*) I'm quite sure she did, yeah.

RUSSELL: Did she demonstrate her love to you?

WILLIAMS: Oh yes, excessively, I should think.

RUSSELL: In what way?

WILLIAMS: I don't know. You can always feel when a mother is excessively concerned for you, you know. And I would cry whenever she left the house and wouldn't stop until she returned. (That was around the age of seven.)

RUSSELL: She was the first person in fact to know you'd won your Theatre Guild prize for $1,000 wasn't she?

WILLIAMS: The Theatre Guild prize? Oh no. What happened was, they'd closed my first play, my first professional play, in Boston; they gave me $100 to go and rewrite it, I don't think *that* would move even Mother to tears. No. The first prize that I got that moved her to tears was a thousand dollars from the Rockefeller Foundation. And she, poor thing, she knew how desperate I was, how unhappy I was at St Louis, and she received the call from New York, and called me to the phone.

I always take these things with outward calm, regardless of how I feel inside, and I said: 'Mother, that was information that I received $1,000 Rockefeller grand!' And she burst into tears, and she said: 'Oh Tom, I'm so happy.'

RUSSELL: You weren't awfully friendly, were you, with your father?

WILLIAMS: Not until after he was dead and then I began to understand him . . .

(*audience laughter*)

RUSSELL: Do you think he did not wish to understand you? Do you think he was unaware of what peculiarity or strangeness lay in his own household?

WILLIAMS: I think he cared for me much more than I knew, but I was named for his father, you see, and he didn't like to see me playing solitary games, you know. I don't refer to onanism, by the way.

RUSSELL: Onanism can be a solitary occupation.

WILLIAMS: Yes, it's solitary if you have any taste! But he didn't like my amusing myself by slapping cards together and imagining the red cards were the Trojans and the black cards were the Greeks.

RUSSELL: He was upset by one thing, wasn't he — when he discovered that you'd written something under a feminine pseudonym?

61

WILLIAMS: Oh yes! (*roaring with laughter*) He was very, very–you wouldn't say martial, but a very, very butch type of man, and he was a man of total honesty. That's the thing I remember about him most.

RUSSELL: What kind of ambitions did he have for you?

WILLIAMS: He wanted me to go into the shoe business, I suppose. He was sales manager of a shoe company.

RUSSELL: Did you ever work in a shoe shop?

WILLIAMS: Three years.

RUSSELL: How did you leave the shoe company? Did you just walk through the door one day?

WILLIAMS: I had a nervous breakdown, with cardiac complications, because I'd stay up all night, drinking black coffee and writing.

RUSSELL: Writing the things you'd been thinking about all through the day?

WILLIAMS: Writing, writing–just writing.

RUSSELL: You cherish your plays still, don't you?

WILLIAMS: Well, it's been my life, yeah.

RUSSELL: But I mean, I'm thinking of why you're here now.

WILLIAMS: I'm here now? I was invited . . . I mean I didn't just barge in. (*audience laughter*)

RUSSELL: Would that you had. Tennessee Williams barging in every night is something. . . .

WILLIAMS: Ah, get out of it.

RUSSELL: What I mean is, when your plays are performed or produced, particularly on this side of the Atlantic and in America, you want to be seen there – not masterminding them, but, but – *supervising* them in the real sense of the word?

WILLIAMS: I want to get a very, *very* powerful director and producer – as I have here with *Streetcar* – and participate slightly in casting, but not have to do anything else.

RUSSELL: Well, when you say not having to do anything else . . . .

WILLIAMS: I concentrate on my writing.

RUSSELL: Now, two or three weeks ago, Gore Vidal, a friend of yours, was a guest on this programme.

WILLIAMS: Very close friend.

RUSSELL: Yes. I gather that, in a conversation with him some time ago you said, apparently, that you had slept throughout the 1960s.

WILLIAMS: I slept through the last six years of them actually, but it could have been the lot.

RUSSELL: And his reply was?

WILLIAMS: 'You didn't miss a thing,' he said.

RUSSELL: Why did you go to sleep for all that time?

WILLIAMS: I was most unhappy during the 'sixties. Things sort of fell apart, you know.

RUSSELL: I mean, you were into a reasonably heavy drug scene then.

WILLIAMS: It doesn't seem to me I drank so terribly much, but I combined it quite frequently with barbiturates, and I was taking speed, to pull myself out of the effects of the liquor and barbiturates. It was, you know, just mad. Now, through with all this, I drink a little water, as you see.

RUSSELL: What helped to pull you out of your bad 'sixties scene?

WILLIAMS: Well, I was committed eventually.

RUSSELL: To a hospital?

WILLIAMS: To a psychiatric hospital, yes. I was committed to the violent ward, although I just sat in the corner reading a book, and trying to avoid the violence that was going on. I saw dreadful things; I saw a man come down the corridor, and another sprang at him and knocked all his teeth out.

Then a girl was brought in—a beautiful girl. She was on an acid trip and she had the most beautiful red hair and I heard her screaming all night. She came out late the next day, with a great bloody bandage around her head and I was told she'd torn her hair out by the roots—all of it. Those are the sort of things that happen there.

RUSSELL: How in hell's name did you survive all that though? And what kept . . .

WILLIAMS: I was determined to get out. You can't stay in a place like that indefinitely, you know.

RUSSELL: How did you persuade one person—if it *was* one person—that you should not be there?

WILLIAMS: Well, there were three doctors; they were neurologists and they had informed my brother that they were the three most eminent neurologists in America. I don't know how they arrived at that conclusion. But my brother was gullible about things; he took their word for it. Eventually, however, they saw that I was not going to succumb—This sounds very paranoiac, doesn't it?—And so I was released eventually. Yeah.

RUSSELL: When you were released, did you suffer a total release of the spirit as well?

WILLIAMS: Oh, I've never had a happier year than 1970. Yeah.

RUSSELL: But did you have a happy first day?

WILLIAMS: Well, it was an enormous relief. I couldn't believe it was true. We came home—I remember my brother drove me to my mother's home. That evening, we sat and watched Vivien Leigh in *The Roman Spring of Mrs Stone*. My mother's a very voluble lady, and she talked all the way through it, and I said: 'Please, mother, I've never seen this film and I love Vivien Leigh. Please let me hear.' She shut up for about a half a minute and then started again.

RUSSELL: Since 1970, has your path been more rosy?

WILLIAMS: Well, the first great sense of release has gone now and I've been caught up again in the travails of showbusiness in America. And it is pretty rough, you know.

RUSSELL: Still, you're used to that arena, aren't you?

WILLIAMS: Oh yes. And I hope that now I can work more in England than in the States.

RUSSELL: Your sister is in a mental hospital, is she not?

WILLIAMS: She has been for many years.

RUSSELL: Do you see her at all?

WILLIAMS: Yes. Once a week — when I'm in the States. She's perfectly able to go out and her reflexes are quicker than mine. She had the first pre-frontal lobotomy — you know what that is? She had one of the first ones performed in America in her twenties. It isn't considered a good therapy any more. It's been almost discredited.

RUSSELL: Is she a happy person?

WILLIAMS: I don't think anyone who is mentally disturbed is happy, no. But she's very brave, enormously brave and dignified.

RUSSELL: When I saw *Streetcar* a week or two ago, I was so . . . pushed over by all sorts of things, but in particular by the New Orleans situation. The south of North America, particularly New Orleans, is a breeding ground for all kinds of things, isn't it?

WILLIAMS: You mean neuroses, things like that?

RUSSELL: Yes. I mean things like faded splendour.

WILLIAMS: Yes, I would say so. But yet I prefer it much to the North. I feel more at home there, because there are more people like me there, you know. 'Faded splendour', did you say? (*laughs*) Society in the South is more homogeneous, and possibly more inbred, than in the North.

RUSSELL: And tragedy seems to be nearer to the surface. People play games more in the South. By that, I mean they play artificial games. They live . . . not artificial lives, but they play parts, almost.

WILLIAMS: I'm not quite sure. They're not quite as interested in baseball as they are in the North! We play a great deal of bridge and poker and, in New Orleans especially, they do an awful lot of drinking.

RUSSELL: And dressing up?

WILLIAMS: Oh yes. And the ladies seem to cultivate a lot more charm there.

RUSSELL: Are they good at freaking out?

WILLIAMS: They freak – you never know whether they're sane or insane. You can't tell.

RUSSELL: Do you think therefore if you'd been born say, in Chicago or Boston or somewhere smart North, you would have gone under?

WILLIAMS: I don't think I would have done very well, because in the South there's a tradition of talking, of expressing oneself, and I listen a great deal and I picked up their way of speech.

RUSSELL: Now, there may be a few people watching tonight who won't ever have heard of you before, or seen you before. They've heard us talk about drugs and alcohol, and the difficulties you've encountered in your life. What they may not know after all that is that as far as your writing is concerned – the actual act of writing – you are a highly disciplined gentleman.

WILLIAMS: I work every day, yes . . . just as long as I possibly can, because I love to. It's my way of life.

RUSSELL: And you get a kick, or a high, out of writing still?

WILLIAMS: Oh yes, oh yes. I love it. Sometimes it goes better than others. It goes better when I'm living a healthy life (coughs), and swimming daily too. That's why Key West is a good place to work. I have my studio and my swimming pool right by my cottage – it's really just a cottage. It's white frame with red shutters – but the garden is what I chiefly like.

RUSSELL: You do it yourself?

WILLIAMS: No, I have a gardener who occupies the house and protects it from looting, you know. I have some good paintings; I think they're good. They're not named paintings, only one of them is by a named painter, but I'm very attached to them.

RUSSELL: Now sexually you said – you said on more than one occasion, you covered the waterfront.

WILLIAMS: Only on one occasion.

RUSSELL: On one occasion – on one memorable occasion.

WILLIAMS: David Frost, yes.

RUSSELL: To name but three.

WILLIAMS: Oh, to name but three (laughs). Well, he comes on like gangbusters. What he said that really hurt me was not 'Was I a homosexual?' – that didn't bother me at all, because I *have* covered the waterfront. Up till I was twenty-eight I was AC/DC, whatever you say – I don't know. Doesn't seem to make any difference – as long as you love, that's the important thing.

RUSSELL: Which is what I was hoping that I might hear you say.

WILLIAMS: Yes. But what he said that I hated was what he said to me shortly after the programme started: 'How do you feel about yourself?' I did not answer him and I looked perplexed and he said: 'Do you like yourself?' I still didn't know how to answer. And he said: 'Do you adore yourself?' I laughed like hell. I said: 'Well, I'm stuck with myself.' That was the real clinker, the real bump. As for the 'I covered the waterfront', I guess that's a funny remark, yes?

RUSSELL: But I'm glad in a sense that the fact that somebody who can cover the waterfront can also celebrate the complexities of people's lives, which your plays do. You bring—I think, I suspect—a lot of hope to people. Are you aware of that?

WILLIAMS: I get a great many letters, yes. I receive letters from people who don't know me much better than the notices I get in America, you know.

RUSSELL: Now, how old are you now?

WILLIAMS: I'll be sixty-three on 26th April.

RUSSELL: Do you feel that you're open to fewer tensions and fewer strains now that you are in your sixties?

WILLIAMS: I've learned to live with them better, yes. You know, you get used to them. A friend of mine kept a diary of her experiences being in Rome with me in 1954, and it seems to me I was much, much more paranoiac and ridiculous then than I am now. . . . I don't have that much of my life left to worry about, you know (laughs).

RUSSELL: Do you intend to squeeze the joyous grape till your last moment?

WILLIAMS: Indeed. Yes, yes.

RUSSELL: Whom would you choose to write your obituary?

WILLIAMS: I would have no control over that. I only hope it's not written by Time magazine (laughs)! It's not that I don't think they do a wonderful job of news reporting. It's just that they have written the worst review about a play of mine and I have the memory of an elephant about a really vicious notice. I'll never forget it.

RUSSELL: I would have thought that a person of your eminence might well be beyond that now though.

WILLIAMS: Oh, I get more vulnerable all the time as far as notices are concerned.

RUSSELL: Thank you for talking with us tonight.

WILLIAMS: It's a pleasure. Thank you.

(applause)

MICHAEL CAINE

RUSSELL: More has been written about the private life of my next guest than he has had private life. In the 1960s his name was never out of the gossip columns; now he's gone legitimate and got himself married. He's a film star. His name is Maurice Joseph Micklewhite. We know him better as superstar Michael Caine.

(*music; applause*)

Got your name right, did I – eventually?

CAINE: Maurice Joseph Micklewhite. Yes, that's it.

RUSSELL: And you were born, so I gather, not a stone's throw from where we are sitting now.

CAINE: We're on the South Bank. I was born at the Elephant and Castle, which is about five minutes down the road.

(*excerpt from* Sleuth*; applause*)

RUSSELL: I have to tell you and everybody else *Sleuth* is a most difficult film to talk about for people who haven't seen it.

CAINE: Yeah. It's very difficult. If I say anything, it gives the game away on the plot. When it was a play it won every prize possible as one of the best thrillers of all time. When I saw the play, I know I was fooled by it completely, and we're hoping most people will be.

RUSSELL: I'm sure they will be. We can't talk about the plot, but we can talk about the fact that you work extensively in the film with Olivier, which was what kind of experience?

CAINE: Well, it's rather like skating with Sonja Henie – the fact that you can do it isn't going to get you very far. Olivier in my own mind is the greatest actor in the world. I was asked for – by him – I mean he got the picture first . . . and then he asked for me. So I turned up on the first day of rehearsals, very much in kind of fear and trembling, but he put me at my ease very fast.

RUSSELL: Were there any difficulties?

CAINE: Well, you imagine the difference between Olivier and I – you know, a theatrical lord and me wandering in. But we had both got to do the same job.

RUSSELL: Yes, but you've notched up as much film experience as he has.

CAINE: That's why we were in a movie and not in a play, because I would never have done a play with him, because he knows more about theatre than anybody.

RUSSELL: The dialogue is actually very exciting in *Sleuth*, isn't it? I mean . . .

CAINE: Fabulous . . . great lines . . .

RUSSELL: Shaffer is a very considerable writer.

CAINE: Well, besides this being a thriller, there are all the class kind of lines and the class things in it which sometimes, for me, were kind of enjoyable to do. I mean, that little sequence we just saw with Larry, sometimes I could hear the sort of lines used by half the people I've lived next door to all my life.

RUSSELL: Do you call him Larry?

CAINE: Yeah. Before I was going to do the film I knew he'd been Sir Laurence Olivier, and then I thought I was going to say Sir Laurence because that's easy.

RUSSELL: And touch your forelock.

CAINE: . . . and then I found out he'd become Lord Olivier, which then threw me into a large investigation into *Burke's Peerage* . . . just to find out who was the Burke,

(*audience laughter*)

and I found out you had to call him My Lord. So I thought: I can't do that! You know, especially in the morning. The take goes wrong on Monday morning and you say: 'Excuse me, my lord.' (Usually, the remark's a bit stronger than that.)

(*audience laughter*)

But fortunately for me, I got a letter – I'd never met Larry – and I had a letter from him which said how happy he was we were working together, and how he was looking forward to it. In the last line, he said that two minutes after we meet we will never call each other anything but christian names again – and it was just signed 'Larry'. So I knew which name he wanted me to say. From then on I called him Larry and he called me Michael, and that was it.

RUSSELL: Very often in the course of the film, he really does go for you, and there's a class distinction between you. This isn't giving anything in the plot away.

CAINE: No.

RUSSELL: How autobiographical do you think that was? Did that unnerve you, or did you get accommodated to it?

CAINE: Well, I thought it was very good, because the class that Larry was playing, he *is*. And the class that the insults were directed at, *I* am. So it was very handy to be able to fall back on real things and real hatreds. I always read about actors who are the part in the evenings, you know. I'm never the part in the evenings and obviously neither is he, because we were great friends. But suddenly this class battle would go on in front of the cameras, which I rather enjoyed because there were times when I could really use it—and really throw it. You know, sometimes you are bottled up all your life.

It's sometimes the way black people get, except they kick holes in television-shop windows and steal a set. But I don't have to do that—that's a catharsis. I think it's great . . .

RUSSELL: You put the catharsis before the horse. (*Caine laughs*) But you don't consider yourself in any way a persecuted minority, do you?

CAINE: Oh no, no, no, no.

RUSSELL: I have heard you once on record, somewhere, saying you thought . . .

CAINE: . . . It's worse than that, we are the persecuted *majority*, for pete's sake. How stupid can you get?

RUSSELL: Who? Who are we talking about?

CAINE: Well, the working class. We're always the persecuted majority. That's really stupid. Fancy being a majority and you're persecuted.

RUSSELL: But that's a sign of the stupidity of the majority.

CAINE: That's what I'm saying. That's what I'm saying: how stupid we were for four hundred years in this country. That's why the majority of people in this country have always been working class—of which I'm one. And, for me, to have been persecuted by, say, an aristocracy, who invented themselves . . .

RUSSELL: But wait a minute—you are now a member of the new aristocracy, aren't you? I mean, you would have to acknowledge that—you're famous.

CAINE: It's got nothing to do with class, or wealth. You have a million dollars and make the wrong sort of thing, like sausages or something, and try and get in the Enclosure at Ascot. Or try and get out of it . . .

(*audience laughter*)

That's what I spend my time doing. The standards were invented by a group of people in this country in particular. In the first place, while everybody was standing around trying to figure out how to read, they got that straight, and then invented themselves.

(*audience laughter*)

'What do you want to be called?' 'I'll be called a Duke, that's kind of nice . . .' 'You know, I'll be a Lord. Yes, Lord.' 'And I'll have a thing with a sable over me, and then when someone who can't read or write sees me, they say, 'Jesus, he must be somebody!', and so it went on like that. I'm here to prove those days are over.

RUSSELL: To switch tracks a bit: who is the most difficult person you've worked with, lady or gentleman? I mean – *do* give names away.

CAINE: The most difficult? I always heard about this when I was a young actor and I was just a young soldier. I used to read how stars were kind of difficult and they had to have certain things . . . but I've never come across any of that. I think Olivier is one of the biggest stars in the world. I mean, he is so easy to work with it's ridiculous. Who have I just worked with? Elizabeth Taylor. She's easy to work with.

RUSSELL: Easy?

CAINE: Yes.

RUSSELL: Well, I've read an article which claims she's anything but easy to work with. In fact, when she was making the Harlech film [*Divorce His, Divorce Hers*] there, she kept coming over in a helicopter or in an aeroplane and buzzing the scenes that Richard Burton was playing so that it would make a noise to distract the public's attention from him.

(*audience laughter*)

CAINE: Oh no – she gets difficult about some things. I remember when we were at Shepperton making *Zee & Co* the Playboy Club were making *Macbeth* (they backed *Macbeth*). Anyway, I remember coming back from lunch one day with her in the car from a pub we used to go to in Shepperton. As we were going through the gates to the studio there was one of these Playboy bunny flags flying over the gate, you know, where the Union Jack used to be. And she said, 'Stop the car.' Then she said, 'Pull that down.' And the gateman said 'But it belongs to Mr Hefner. Playboy is making a film here, and that's the flag.' She said, 'Just put the flag up over their stage, but not over the studio. *I* don't work under the bunny flag.' – which she doesn't.

RUSSELL: Is she a tough lady?

CAINE: She's tough if *you* want to be tough. She's like a real fighter. When Cassius Clay – Mohammed Ali – walks into a room, he doesn't have to say 'I'm going to punch somebody's head in in here.' He just doesn't have to say it. Well, I mean, from a work point of view, Elizabeth can punch anybody's head in. But she doesn't have to say it. So, she's never temperamental.

RUSSELL: How much danger is there, do you think, of your getting into that kind of bracket, where you're isolated maybe from your own self-critical apparatus?

CAINE: No danger at all. 'Cos she's a really, really great star, you know, of the old, real Hollywood school. Even if I had the kind of personality that makes that kind of star, I've missed the boat anyway, because that kind of Hollywood thing has gone.

RUSSELL: You're heading fairly rapidly up that ladder now.

CAINE: Yes, but this is just an actor thing. You see, you could be a star like that not really doing anything. See some of the old films that your mum and dad told you were great, see the actors that they said were marvellous. They say: 'You don't get them like that any more.' Watch 'em on the late, late show. You've seen 'em. You'll be glad you *don't* get 'em like that any more.

(*audience laughter*)

Those guys were made stars by the studios. And Elizabeth was made a star by the studio, and in actual fact didn't like it, and got out of it. She's a very genuine lady, actually.

RUSSELL: Because you're heading up the superstar bracket, that means you get mobbed and pushed at, and pulled at, in public. Does that happen to you at all?

CAINE: No, never. I've never managed to cause hysteria anywhere.

(*audience laughter*)

RUSSELL: Have you been offered the centre spread of *Cosmopolitan* yet?

CAINE: No. Not yet. I doubt whether I ever will. I don't even have the upper for that, let alone the lower.

(*wild laughter*)

I'd rather put a vest on, and socks, and leave the rest.

RUSSELL: A stapling machine could come in handy though, on the centre spread.

CAINE: That's what worries me about that stapler . . . makes your eyes water.

RUSSELL: I was a bit amazed to find, in the film *Sleuth*, to find that you were wearing those baggy boxer shorts.

CAINE: Yes, you always have to wear those. I normally wear those — er — what do you call them?—'Y-fronts', but you can't wear those in the movie, they said.

RUSSELL: Why?

CAINE: You've got to wear something a little more baggy, see, because you mustn't give the plot away.

(*audience laughter*)

RUSSELL: Talking of the intimate details of your person brings me almost to the intimate details of your personality: you've got married again recently.

CAINE: Yeah, I got married again after, what – twelve years. You make it sound like a . . .

RUSSELL: I meant that you're still believing in the state of matrimony . . . as an institution.

CAINE: I believe in it for me at certain times. If we've got to have a baby, then we get married. That's how it worked out. If I was in love with somebody, I wouldn't get married just because I was in love with somebody. I don't see that side of it at all.

RUSSELL: But you are a one-woman man, aren't you?

CAINE: I always have been. I tried hard, but couldn't make it (*laughs*). I always wound up as a kind of one-woman man. I've never regarded myself as a bachelor . . . I've always regarded myself as a man who hadn't married yet.

RUSSELL: If you are made Lord Caine, may I still call you Michael?

CAINE: It's highly unlikely – a very unlikely hypothesis – is that the word?

RUSSELL: It's a big word to finish with. Michael Caine, thank you very much indeed.

(*applause*)

GORE VIDAL

RUSSELL: My first guest tonight is someone who believes that the human race is rumbling downhill to its destruction with ever-increasing speed; he believes that babies should be born only under licence, and he confesses that he cannot understand why people fall in love with each other. His name, welcome him, is Gore Vidal.

(*music; applause*)

GORE VIDAL: That is the most extraordinary introduction I have ever heard.

RUSSELL: Why?

GORE VIDAL: I certainly understand why people fall in love with one another: — mirrors.

RUSSELL: Mirrors?

GORE VIDAL: Yes (*laughs*).

RUSSELL: Do you use a mirror at all?

GORE VIDAL: Just to shave.

RUSSELL: But when you shave, do you ever fall in love with yourself?

GORE VIDAL: No, . . . there are two kind of narcissus, there is the objective, and the subjective. The subjective looks in the mirror, like this, and says, 'It's never been more beautiful'; the objective says 'It's never been such a ruin'. I'm the objective; I see the destruction.

RUSSELL (*laughs*): Are you able to take steps to repair it? You've had a lot of practice, this last two or three weeks, chatting, talking, being around, haven't you? I mean, you appear to have been . . .

GORE VIDAL: 'Over-exposed' is the word. That's quite true, yes.

RUSSELL: Well, if you're over-exposed, I'd like to be talking tonight about things you haven't discussed already. You've talked at some length about the election which you were involved in . . . as a commentator.

GORE VIDAL: I felt towards the end as though I were standing. At three in the morning the returns are coming in, from Baxter-on-Sea Sea . . .

RUSSELL: From where?

GORE VIDAL (*laughs*): I just invented it: maybe there is a Baxter-on-Sea, and I am the member. Now, a few words to those of you who helped me on this campaign . . .

RUSSELL: Did you like all the mayors?

GORE VIDAL: The mayors were wonderful. In America, our mayors are very different, of course, A great many of them are in prison or on their way. But they wear sort of lumpy suits, and don't have chains of office. I think maybe the fact that in England you give them chains of office keeps them from taking money. This may very well be an insight into the difference between your country and ours. I'd like you to think about that.

(*audience laughter*)

RUSSELL: Do you mean, if we dress ourselves in brief authority it prevents us from being naughty?

GORE VIDAL: Yes. I think also that to pay people in honour, rather than in money, is a very clever system, particularly when your island keeps running out of money. It is much better to be called Sir Something Something at the end of thirty years than to be living in Argentina with a rather nice fortune, as I suspect our President will be presently when Congress is through with him.

(*audience laughter*)

RUSSELL: Do you ever imagine yourself, . . . well, first of all, do you fantasise?

GORE VIDAL: About what? At the moment I have a passion, and that is the Earl of Longford, with whom I debated the other night. I'm really in love with him – he's every bit as nice as he looks. He's rather marvellous, so I've been the Earl of Longford for about three days now. I've been going to Soho, into the porn shops, and telling them, 'Get those things out of my sight!' It's been my Lord Longford week, but next week, I might be somebody else.

RUSSELL: If you were to be adopted as an English citizen, would you crave an honour?

GORE VIDAL: I don't think so, no. It depends on what age you are. If you were young, of course that's very attractive, but after a while – I suppose as you work, and as you make your own name – the idea of a title sounds diminishing. That is, Sir Winston Churchill always sounded wrong. Just plain Winston Churchill had a great ring to it, and I always thought he rather diminished himself, taking the Garter, or whatever it was, that gave him this title.

RUSSELL: 'Lord Gore Vidal', though, has a kind of resonance about it, hasn't it? A kind of majesty?

GORE VIDAL: Yes, I sort of feel like a large painting, slowly ageing away (*laughs*).

RUSSELL: Now, if you'll forgive me, there may be people watching this programme, tonight . . .

GORE VIDAL: Or again, there may not be! I would not be optimistic at all.

(*audience laughter*)

RUSSELL (*laughing*): . . . who just may not have heard of Gore Vidal, or know what Gore Vidal does.

GORE VIDAL: Well, by now they would have turned off.

(*audience laughter*)

RUSSELL: Well, just in case there are two, lingering somewhere, wondering what the hell's going on, can I myself offer to them a small resumé of certain things?

GORE VIDAL: Yes.

RUSSELL: You're the person who scandalised America by knocking the Kennedys when it wasn't fashionable. You're the person who appalled the likes of Mary Whitehouse by suggesting that there were only two things in life, at the extreme ends of love, which were lust on the one hand, and compassion; and that love for you didn't exist in the middle. You're the gentlemen who raised the eyebrows of the Western world by recommending orgies as a satisfying sex experience.

GORE VIDAL: Only if you were in good condition. After a certain age, it is unbecoming.

(*audience laughter*)

RUSSELL: (*laughs*) And you're the gentleman who steamed Lord Longford's glasses by proclaiming that you thought the family was out of date.

GORE VIDAL: I think he had his glasses off at that point.

RUSSELL: He didn't take his glasses off – they were on. I was watching, so I know they were on.

GORE VIDAL: I was . . . just trying not to get over-excited looking at him, so I looked over his head . . .

(*audience laughter*)

Now that you've assembled that little series of libels, one by one, which shall we start with? What was No. 1?

RUSSELL: I think we've dealt with No. 1, about the Kennedys. I am much more interested in the personal things, the things that pertain to you, which is your proclamation about lust on the one hand, and compassion on the other.

GORE VIDAL: Well, I think it is as sensible as one sentence can be — which is never very sensible, and never the entire story, of course. Lust is known to all of us; lust is perfectly normal; it is built in. Without it, we would not continue to produce these dismal replicas of ourselves, which are currently eating up the food of the world, taking up space, and running out of oil and such things. So lust is built in. I'd rather see lust used just for itself, for its own sake. This is a new thought to Mrs Whitehouse, and to my new passion, the Earl of Longford, but I think most people realise that lust is not only one of the pleasanter things that we have down here.

Tell you something, the ruling class of England has never wanted the lower orders to have a good time. Do you remember *Lady Chatterley's Lover*? They got very over-excited, you know, when they found out that the gamekeeper was keeping company with Lady Chatterley, in a bosky dell. They didn't like it being a gamekeeper, you know; if it had been her husband's brother, that would have been friendly and aristocratic. So there's always been a sort of class thing here. You don't let the lower orders have any fun. You shut down their bars, so they don't get drunk, so they'll be able to work the next day; you encourage them to get married and have children, because then they're not going to leave their job, are they? They're going to starve to death. You don't encourage them to remain single, because then you haven't got any purchase on them. So it's very much a class thing.

I noticed it with Lord Longford: he kept making exemptions. He was pretty strong in general. He is a devout Roman Catholic and Christian puritan, but he kept saying, 'Well, of course, they're brilliant people', or 'very sophisticated people'. And he's got a thing about the Duke of Wellington. The Duke of Wellington can do no wrong, of course, with his private life.

RUSSELL: This is the first Duke of Wellington?

GORE VIDAL: Well, of course, we don't want to take it off the air in two minutes!

(*audience laughter*)

The first Duke of Wellington's private life was really bad news, according to Lord Longford, though I think he was just great, as Anglo-Irish peers go. But Lord Longford was making, I could tell, a sort of subtle distinction — that it was really all right if you were the Duke of Wellington, but was not all right if you worked in a factory, or on a farm, in which case you really ought to toe the line.

The aristocracy has been getting away with murder on this island, you know. Because they kept a difference between themselves and the others. They never believed, in other words, in Christian puritanism, and that lust was bad, but they managed to create such a response in their serfs.

As for compassion, that is, I think, something that has absolutely nothing to do with sex. Sex is a very good way to get to know people – that's certainly quite true. It's not the only way, and sometimes it is a dead end, as many weeping people of both sexes have discovered. But compassion is simply nothing more than a bit of imagination which is killed in us, usually, very early on. Because if we could really imagine what other people felt like – which isn't very difficult, they don't feel any different from us – we would behave better towards them. But then, if you try to put love in a sexual exclusivity together with compassion, you just end up with what they call the nuclear family unit, reproducing itself at the rate of 2.4, and I think that makes for a lot of unhappiness. Get to No. 3 now, I've run out . . .

RUSSELL: No. 3 was about the recommendation of orgies as a satisfactory sexual act. Is this a satisfactory one for you?

GORE VIDAL: What an unbecoming question to ask!

RUSSELL: Completely natural question, though, isn't it?

GORE VIDAL: Well, it's a flattering question, I'll say that. I haven't been so flattered in a long time. (*Russell laughs.*) Here I am, suffering from dyspepsia, slightly overweight, worrying about my health all the time, and you ask me if I could go to an orgy. I assume this was an invitation I have just got?

(*audience laughter*)

And here I am, just unable to go through with it, you know, because I am not feeling that good. But in my youth, I used to think it was absolutely grand, yes, and you did get to meet a lot of people, that you ordinarily wouldn't know . . .

(*audience laughter*)

RUSSELL: A nice class of person?

GORE VIDAL: Well, you get a better class of person at orgies, because people have to keep in trim more. There is an awful lot of going round holding in your stomach, you know. Everybody is very polite to each other. The conversation isn't very good, but you can't have everything.

(*audience laughter*)

RUSSELL: And you shouldn't speak with your mouth full, as well.

(*wild laughter*)

GORE VIDAL: That'll be cut!

(*audience laughter*)

RUSSELL: Now, are all these things private thoughts of yours, or are you claiming in any sense that they are public proclamations or maybe rules or guidelines which the rest of us should follow, perhaps?

GORE VIDAL: Well, I'm a continuous teacher as a writer and political commentator in the Land of the Free and the Home of the Brave across the ocean, and I'm perfectly willing to do missionary work here, from time to time—but only in the most casual way. I don't prescribe for anybody. I do occasionally draw people's attention to what I think are confusions and sources of unhappiness, and I think we've certainly made a mess out of sex. The only argument for doing it was, of course, that the family was sacred, because we needed more people, because until this century we had an enormous infant mortality rate: you would have fourteen children, of which two would survive. Everybody survives now. And the result is that we're getting a bit crowded. You know, we're running out of food. There are three-and-a-half billion people in the world now, and in thirty-seven years we will have doubled it, and there will be nothing to feed them with.

RUSSELL: You haven't got a family of your own, but do you enjoy sharing other people's family lives?

GORE VIDAL: Well, *you* don't know if I've a family of my own or not. I must say my approach to children is not unlike that of King Herod (*laughs*) . . . but I put up with my friends' children. After they start talking, I get interested in them. But I think that we treat children very badly, all over the West. We ghetto-ise them: children are put with children, youngish people with youngish people, middle-aged people with middle-aged people, old people with old people. There is no longer the interaction that you got when you had a smaller population, and bigger families and bigger houses, with from four generations living in the same house. So children don't get to know anybody but other children, and I'm not awfully impressed with the children I meet, at least around the United States. They're rather sullen, they don't know their parents very well, and what they see of their parents they don't like, and the parents honestly don't like them very much, but everybody puts on a good face. They don't see the grandparents at all because they're living in the sunny acres of the golden retirement years, playing bridge, and it's a sad scene.

RUSSELL: Did you have a happy childhood?

GORE VIDAL: Yes, I think I probably did. There was a lot more room then, when I was a child, at the time of the Boer War!
(*audience laughter*)
There were large houses, and it was very entertaining. I was mostly brought up by my grandparents until I was about ten years old, and I was devoted to them. I am something of a gerontophile; I like older people, which means that as I get older I have less and less company! I shall soon be all alone; Methusaleh. Oh dear!
(*audience laughter*)
RUSSELL: I have the impression, talking to you here, that you are the kind of person who skates very elegantly and beautifully across the top of life, and that you never get caught up in the reed beds that the rest of us are thrashing around in. How do you manage that? Or first of all, do you accept that as a definition?
GORE VIDAL: I have been very fortunate in my life, in that I have lived in many different countries, and many different levels of society, and among many different kinds of people. And so my skating is really an effort to keep up with the human race, which I had the very good fortune to get to know, instead of being stuck, as most people are. I think most people would be very happy to do the skating I do.
RUSSELL: One of the places in the world where it's better to keep up than to be caught in the reed beds must in fact be Italy, mustn't it? Particularly Rome, where you elect to live for some part of your life?
GORE VIDAL: Rome is a good city to live in, though it is not what it was twenty years ago, ten years ago, five years ago. But I still like the Italians. My father's family came from the Italian Alps.
RUSSELL: Is Rome a relaxing sort of city to live in, for you?
GORE VIDAL: Well you know, you make your own life; I could live in Detroit, or Sidcup, for that matter, and lead the same sort of life. My life is reading and writing and seeing. No matter where you live, you only seem to know five people, whether you are living in New York with twelve million people around you, or London, or an Italian town, you only meet, you only see five.
RUSSELL: Do you think you could lead the kind of life that you do, and accomplish so well, without the money and the wealth that you possess?
GORE VIDAL: The money? The wealth I possess! You should see my tax bill! American writers who live abroad, contrary to the legend, must pay full tax. Even though you earn no money in the United States and live abroad — if I never went back for twenty years, I'd

still pay automatically 50 per cent of my income. And as for inherited wealth—I inherited absolutely nothing at all. It's just what I make. Scribble, scribble, scribble!

RUSSELL: Do you like being able to put your hands on—whatever you wish to put your hands on, if you see what I mean?

(*audience laughter*)

Wine, pictures, books, travel?

GORE VIDAL: I like to travel. As a writer you get sent a lot of books which is very helpful. When I was young, I occasionally would take books out of the library and never return them. I have still got some Library of Congress books from forty years ago, when my grandfather was in the Senate, which were never returned. Books are the only possession that I value at all. I was never greedy, which I suspect was why I never had any trouble making money. Because I wasn't interested in that, it came my way.

RUSSELL: Now, you have said a lot of things which are clearly important to you about families, about morality, about the way one behaves. Why, if you believe in these things so strongly, and can express them so forcefully, do you fiddle in Rome while the rest of the world is burning?

GORE VIDAL: Well, I should think that the fiddling makes beautiful music, which I hope is heard everywhere.

RUSSELL: Yes, but a person of your position and power, by which I mean the power of your voice, and the power of your written word, could actually go and knock on the door of Congress, or of the United Nations, and say, 'This is my plan for the terrible situation which I think the world population now is in.' Why don't you do that?

GORE VIDAL: Right. I have been involved in every American election since 1948—ask any American you know, they say terrible things about my involvement. I am always in politics. And I am always doing this sort of thing, but I have to have a place to be sufficiently serene in to write. And that's Rome. I was at one time in active politics, but I decided that one was more useful on the outside, because as a writer you must always tell the truth, or try to. And as a politician, you must never give the game away. These are two absolutely separate things. The only writers who pulled it off as politicians were, I suppose, Disraeli, who wrote before he became Prime Minister, and Churchill, whose books were really sort of journalistic self-advertisements. So he was all of a piece, but he was never telling the truth in the way a writer ought to.

RUSSELL: So you don't feel that you could operate extra-politically without lying, even if you could do it privately?

GORE VIDAL: No. You see, what we have in America, you don't have here. You tend to put everybody in categories. My equivalent over here – I don't know who he'd be . . . somebody like John Osborne, or Kingsley Amis, or whatever . . . You accept them as people who can comment on a scene only as long as they're jokes. If they get serious, then you say, 'What does a mere writer know?' To which my answer is, 'What does a mere solicitor know?' That's all he was, or an advertising man, God forbid, which many of them were. In America, people like Mailer and myself and James Baldwin are not so humble, and we go out getting enormous audiences. I've just come from fifteen cities in the United States suggesting, as amiably as I can, that the country would be happier with Richard Nixon in Louisberg Federal Penitentiary. With our election, I get three or four thousand people, and Mailer can do the same. I think it is a pity that your writers, who are certainly as bright, if not brighter, than we are, have accepted their role. When John Osborne or somebody attacked the monarchy two years ago, the Press played it up, and made him look silly. And he is not a silly man at all. So I suggest to my confreres over here that they might get cracking and get serious.

RUSSELL: Is Richard Nixon afraid of you in any way, do you think?

GORE VIDAL: I wouldn't say. He has so much to fear now. Along the way, he has responded to my criticism. I have gone on television very often, after he has finished a speech, to point out the mendacity of his views. He is very spontaneous about it. It is quite wonderful.

RUSSELL: You mean a spontaneous liar?

GORE VIDAL: Yes, it is quite extraordinary! He will even tell a lie when it is not convenient to.

(*audience laughter*)

That is the sign of a great artist, you know.

RUSSELL: Let us finally speculate one thing. Suppose that what you predict happens to Richard Nixon, and supposing some gentlemen got themselves together, and said, 'The only person who can save this country is called Vidal, and he lives in Rome. Come back, Gore, all is forgiven.' Would you willingly wing your way across the Atlantic?

GORE VIDAL: You assume that I have not been elected Pope at this point?

(*audience laughter*)

As long as we're going to fantasise, that is a little more exciting to me.

RUSSELL: You would rather be a Pope?

GORE VIDAL: Oh, my heavens! Can't you see me on the balcony, talking about contraception?

(*roars of laughter*)

I might save humanity – at least I could save Latin America! My Papacy is what I'm really looking forward to. I did think very much about the American Presidency as a person in a political family. But we live in dangerous times, and I could see myself perhaps being elected and rapidly ending up in a box at Arlington cemetery, because that's what we do to our politicians who promise change. Luckily, your politicians never promise change, so they're perfectly safe to go on talking!

(*audience laughter*)

RUSSELL: But I do cherish the vision of you on the balcony of San Pietro, with your mitre – or is it the papal crown?

GORE VIDAL: Yes, it's a triple tiara. But I would wear the ordinary white cap: the white beanie, as we call it in America.

RUSSELL: Would there be a job for me in the College of Cardinals?

GORE VIDAL: I should think, no. But there's a very good sort of Irish Catholic order that looks after the catacombs. They're all from Dublin, and you could be a very good MC, because they have a lot of jokes, as they take people through to show them the skeletons. I could fix you up there.

(*audience laughter*)

RUSSELL: Well, . . . I was going to say I'm used to playing to a large dead section of the population, but I won't say it.

GORE VIDAL: Let us rise up now! I wouldn't take that from him! Really!

RUSSELL: I take it all back.

GORE VIDAL: Absolutely. Bite the hand that does not applaud you!

(*audience laughter*)

RUSSELL: From which hands I will now request applause for Gore Vidal.

(*applause*)

JEAN MARSH

RUSSELL: My first guest tonight had a beautiful idea in the bath –
in a swimming bath as a matter of fact. It was the original idea from
which one of the most successful television shows emerged. The
show is *Upstairs, Downstairs* – and the lady who thought of it is the
lovely Rose, from this programme. Ladies and gentlemen, Miss
Jean Marsh.

(*music from* Upstairs, Downstairs; *applause*)

RUSSELL: You were in a swimming bath when you had this bright
idea.

JEAN: Mmm. Yes.

RUSSELL: That's not a story you've manufactured – that's for real,
is it?

JEAN: Oh no, that's absolutely true. I was away on holiday with
Eileen Atkins and we were staying at a friend's house in the South of
France – P-P-Paddy Campbell. We were standing in his swimming
pool. And I said, 'I must have more of this. I must have more of
swimming pools and South of France and things like this', and she
said, 'Well, you'll need money', and so we just started thinking, you
know, about money and general ways to make it, and then we were
talking about our backgrounds, which are both very similar. We
both come from poor families, and poor parts of London, and we
both have a parent who was in service, and it just evolved gradually
from that. Flew back to London, and sold it.

RUSSELL: Yes, but it wasn't – it couldn't all have been as easy as that.
Could it?

JEAN: Well – I – it'll annoy everybody, but it was *terribly* easy. When
we came back to London I wrote it down quite carefully, and an
outline, and ideas for casting, things like that, and then we didn't do
anything about it immediately. One day I was out of work and
feeling a bit glum, and a girl-friend rang me. She was very beautiful
and very rich, and married to an attractive man, had a house on the
river and two children, and she was working. It made me so angry
that I called up the production company, and said 'I've got an idea

83

for a television series', and told it to them, and they said, 'Well, we'll call you back in a couple of weeks probably.' They called back in half an hour . . .

RUSSELL: Oh really?

JEAN: And said, would I have lunch with them? — which I did. And at lunch-time they said they would buy it, and about two or three days later, London Weekend Television bought the idea. I mean, it was *very* quick and very easy (*laughing*).

RUSSELL: Sounds *too* easy, doesn't it?

JEAN: Yes. I don't think it'll ever happen again.

RUSSELL: Yes — the whole audience is about to rush out from this studio and get into a swimming bath and start having ideas.

(*audience laughter*)

JEAN: Oh do. Do. I mean, maybe it'll work for everybody.

RUSSELL: Let me be saucy and ask you what you were doing immediately before you got into your bath and had a beautiful thought? . . . I don't mean that day, I mean . . .

JEAN: No, no. Well, I've always been an actress, so I had been acting, but not with enormous success. I think just before that I'd been doing a series, again here, called *The Informer* with Ian Hendry and Heather Sears, and . . . odd plays. I just drifted around. I've never been very ambitious.

RUSSELL: But was it a roughish life? I mean did you have to work hard to get work?

JEAN: I do *look* a bit rough now.

RUSSELL: No! No!

JEAN: No? I've never been a great star, you know, I've never been very ambitious but I was pushed at an early age to be an actress, and I've been an actress since I was seven — of sorts — an extra, not a child star, and I think it's been simple but not terribly good.

RUSSELL: Right.

JEAN: And I've had lucky things happen to me, like I worked in America simply because the major casting woman there, Rose Tobias Shaw, happened to see me in a restaurant and said, 'I like that girl's face'; and then I worked for three years in America doing very good work, from chance.

RUSSELL: What kind of service was your mother in?

JEAN: She was not a housemaid, more of a tweeny, because she left quite young. She didn't stay in service. She stepped up in the world and became a barmaid — which seems funny now, but it was an improvement.

RUSSELL: What did your father do when you were a child?

JEAN: He was a printer's assistant – you hump bits of machinery around in the print.

RUSSELL: But was it a poor household?

JEAN: Oh yes, we were very poor.

RUSSELL: And yet, you see, behind all that there is obviously a feeling for words, and a feeling for the drama, and a feeling for the things which you wouldn't automatically expect to spring out of a poor working-class background.

JEAN: Well, that's grown up with time. But – I'm very lucky, my parents were quite unusual inasmuch as they always had very good books around. I mean, the first book I read was Jane Austen. And always very good music, so that was a little different.

RUSSELL: Did she borrow them from 'upstairs'?

JEAN (*laughing*): No, they were bought I think, or stolen! I don't know. But that made a difference.

RUSSELL: But your Dad had something to do with the pub, didn't he?

JEAN: No, no. I bet you read that in a paper.

RUSSELL: I did.

JEAN: These journalists are extraordinary. You spend hours talking to them. They get it all wrong. My father has supported a brewery all his life . . .

(*audience laughter*)

but – he's never *worked* in one. I now live in one, in fact. . . . It's not a pub any more, but my house in the country was a pub. It's still got a beer pump down to the cellar.

RUSSELL: How lovely! Do you use it?

JEAN: No, I don't drink beer. I only drink champagne.

(*audience laughter*)

RUSSELL: Well, you can pump *that*! I imagine that champagne would go through a tube as easily as beer.

JEAN: It goes down *me* too quickly to get down to the cellar.

RUSSELL: What kind of school days did you enjoy? I mean, *were* they enjoyable or were they tedious?

JEAN: Well, no – in fact, I would have loved to have stayed at school. I mean, I would have liked to have gone to university – I was a very academic little girl. I would have preferred that really to acting. I adored being at ordinary school but when I was quite young – nine or ten – they sent me to a dancing school that had education thrown in, and I hated dancing. So really my education stopped when I was about ten.

RUSSELL: I also get feelings from you, from talking with you previously that you're also a kind of learned lady in a way, aren't you? You're a bit blue in the stocking.

JEAN: Oh very—yes very. Very blue stocking. I read a lot. (*Whispers*) Don't watch television very much (*laughing*).

RUSSELL (*also whispering*): Do you watch *Upstairs, Downstairs?*

JEAN: Yes. I love *Upstairs, Downstairs*. It's the only thing I've ever been in that I watch, and I just watch it as a play, for pleasure. I don't watch *me*.

RUSSELL: You're short-sighted, perhaps that's why . . .

(*audience laughter*)

JEAN: Oh, I think that's rude!

RUSSELL: No, no, no. You caused a hell of a lot of havoc with *Upstairs, Downstairs* . . . people say to me, 'Who have you got on the programme this week?' or 'Who's on next week?' or whatever it is, and I have said once or twice to people this week 'I'm going to be talking with Jean Marsh'.

JEAN: Oh, I bet they didn't know Jean Marsh.

RUSSELL: Oh yes, yes they did, yes they did. And they said, 'Well, we know who *she* is because she's the girl who sat on an egg which eventually became *Upstairs, Downstairs*, and she's Rose, and everything. And (this is in a pub actually)—and the landlord said, 'We don't like her very much round here', and I said, 'Why?' and he said, 'Because when *Upstairs, Downstairs* is on, the bleeding pub's empty.'

(*audience laughter*)

JEAN: Really?

RUSSELL: The telly's up there and everybody's facing that way watching *Upstairs, Downstairs* and you know . . .

JEAN: And they're not buying the booze. Oh, that's very good. I'm very pleased to hear it.

RUSSELL: So. Well it's pleasurable for you, but the pub-keeper was a bit angry.

JEAN: Well, I mean, I can't worry about him, he's got to look after his own business. Maybe he should get an idea about a pub being a central part of a television series.

(*audience laughter*)

RUSSELL: Are you recognised a lot now?

JEAN: Yes. But people don't usually know my name. I mean, they shout 'Hullo, Rose'. You know. I mean the difference between a film-star and a television star is if people see Elizabeth Taylor walking

Above Gary Glitter

Below April Ashley
with Russell

Above Barry Humphries (Edna Everage)

Below Russell with Frankie Howerd

Above Barbara Cartland

Below John Osborne, Jill Bennett

Above Elton John

Below Ilie Nastase and Russell

Above Molly Parkin

Below David Niven
with Russell

Above Joan Marsh, Russell

Below Jeanette Charles taking tea with Russell

Above Dame Sybil
Thorndike

Below Oliver Reed
and Russell

Above Ringo Starr

Below June Havoc
with Russell

down the street they say, 'Oh look, there's Elizabeth Taylor.' If they see me they say, 'Oh look, there's what'shername.'

(*audience roars with laughter*)

RUSSELL: But it *happens*. It happens in foreign lands now, I hear.

JEAN: Yes. It happened in Berlin a few months ago. I was there doing a film, because I speak a little German you see. I am very . . . clever . . .

RUSSELL: Blue in the stocking . . .

JEAN: I was walking down the Kurfürstendamm, which is like Oxford Street, and somebody shouted 'Hullo, Rosa'. That was very odd.

RUSSELL: How did they know you there? They'd seen you here, presumably.

JEAN: Oh, they'd seen me here.

RUSSELL: Does it get piped abroad a lot?

JEAN: We've sold very well abroad. Yes, in fact we've just sold to America, which is very nice.

RUSSELL: No wonder your eyes are like cash registers.

(*audience laughter*)

JEAN: We don't make *that* much money.

RUSSELL: You don't! How long do you think you're going to go on being in – quotes – 'service' – unquote?

JEAN: Ah well, it's difficult to say because I own it, as it were, and it's my idea. I'd feel very disloyal if I left. If it wasn't my idea I wouldn't go on with it, but I'm going to do another series and then we'll see.

RUSSELL: Does Eileen Atkins regret not being in it?

JEAN: Oh I think she would have liked to, but – the week we started rehearsing she opened in *Vivat, Vivat Regina*, and it's always very difficult for her. She's always booked so far ahead – I mean she's our greatest actress of her age, you know. A far greater actress than me – or indeed I think any of the other – you know . . .

RUSSELL: Whom you will not name at this time?

JEAN: Well, V.R., M.S. . . . (*laughing*). I think we've got a lot of great actresses in their thirties, but I think Eileen is the best, and so she works a lot.

RUSSELL: It would have been a very interesting sort of arrangement – you and her, if she was upstairs, say, or she were to . . .

JEAN: Well no, we were both going to be maids.

RUSSELL: You were?

JEAN: Well, one of the reasons we did think of the idea was, we wanted to change our parts, because normally all my work, in spite of being a scrubber, all my work has been as ladies. It usually says 'Lydia glides on looking romantically pretty', or something, and I just longed, you know, to use my own accent.

RUSSELL: Do you get mail – agony letters, or mail from people wanting help because of the predicaments that they're in?

JEAN: Well – I do. I get more letters about interviews in newspapers than about situations in the series. I get a lot of mail from men whose wives have left them, and I can't quite work out why. I mean, maybe they think I'd be a good cook and look after them, or something . . . which I am – a very good cook.

RUSSELL: You're a very 'neat' lady.

JEAN: Sounds a bit dull.

RUSSELL: No, it's not dull, but you are together. I presume you're together at home . . . you do the cooking, and I bet all your books are in alphabetical order . . .

JEAN: Oh no, they're not. But my drawers are clean and tidy – I mean my . . .

(audience roars with laughter)

JEAN: They are too, of course. Yes, I'm quite – I'm quite ordered. I have to be, because I work very hard. I also write a lot now – and I've got other ideas, and you see I've got a lot to do.

RUSSELL: Well now, wait a minute before you go. If you have other ideas, and if you ever feel as though you're going to slide into somebody's swimming-pool, would you take me with you?

JEAN: Yes. I would anyway, actually.

RUSSELL: Thank you very much, Jean Marsh.

(applause)

JILL BENNETT AND JOHN OSBORNE

RUSSELL: My next guest has a taste for champagne in the small hours of the morning, set off sometimes with a small tin of new potatoes, and so she keeps a refrigerator at her bedside. She's Miss Jill Bennett . . .

(*music; applause*)

Now, is it true about the new potatoes in . . . in the bedroom?

JILL: Oh, yes. . . . Delicious. I eat them all the time – *and* veal and ham pie, actually.

(*audience laughter*)

RUSSELL: In the middle of the night.

JILL: Yes, in the middle of the night.

RUSSELL: Does that mean that you sleep badly?

JILL: I sleep badly, but I don't need much sleep. I like getting up in the night. I'm a night bird, really.

RUSSELL: Do you sleep without pyjamas, or do you have a sort of frilly thing on?

JILL: Not frilly. I have a sort of rather plain, dreary sort of spinsterish nightgown.

RUSSELL: And you get out and get the tin opener.

JILL: When I'm not on my bicycle, yes.

(*audience laughter*)

RUSSELL: I think I ought to explain what you're talking about with bicycles.

JILL: Yes.

RUSSELL: Because there was an unfortunate episode with a bike, wasn't there?

JILL: Yes, I did go out on my bicycle in a nightdress and I was riding round the square, I think with one of my dogs in the basket, on the wrong side of the road. And a policeman found me and caught me and brought me home and gave me some tea. I think he thought I was quite mad. I probably was, of course.

RUSSELL: Was it because you just felt like going for a ride on a bike, or were you sleep cycling?

89

JILL: Oh no, I wanted to go for a ride on a bike. And it seemed rather pleasant out. I think I'd had a bit to drink too, mind you, and I felt rather jolly. I don't think John was there so I had no one to talk to. I can't wake him up and talk to him all night . . .

RUSSELL: Is he a better sleeper than you?

JILL: Oh yes, but he wouldn't admit to it.

RUSSELL: You have said to me privately that you are a very nervous lady.

JILL: Yes.

RUSSELL: Are you nervous at this moment?

JILL: Absolutely terrified, yes. But I'm quite enjoying it too.

RUSSELL: Are you?

JILL: I think I enjoy being nervous. I mean I wouldn't be an actress otherwise. But I am very nervous.

RUSSELL: You're collecting very good notices and doing very good business with your appearance in *Private Lives*, which I enjoyed hugely. A very different performance from M. Smith.

JILL: Mmm.

RUSSELL: Did you see her performance before you went?

JILL: No, because I was asked not to by the director – John Gielgud – because he thought it might sort of worry and unstabilise me, and also he redirected it really.

RUSSELL: But surely you've been bombarded by people coming up to you and saying, 'She didn't do it like that, she did this'?

JILL: No, not very much actually, except when we were rehearsing business which had obviously taken months to work out. But never in a nasty sort of way.

RUSSELL: How long ago did you know that you might be destined to take that role?

JILL: Quite a bit ago, when they knew she was going to leave. John Gielgud rang me up, and I decided not to, because I was too nervous. But my friend John Osborne made me do it. He said it would be good for me to get away from his plays and do something funny. Quite right too.

RUSSELL: John Gielgud . . . you've had a close relationship with him for many years?

JILL: Yes.

RUSSELL: Is it true that he pointed at you on a stage a long time ago, before you weren't what you are now?

JILL: Yes (*laughs*). I was walking-on when I was seventeen at Stratford, in *Much Ado About Nothing* and there were some lilies that somebody had to carry and he said, 'That girl, the one with the strange face, she can carry them.' That was probably a compliment. At the time I was in despair. He doesn't remember doing it though. But, you know, I don't think he's a brick-dropper, I think he tells some rather good truths, you know.

RUSSELL: You don't think he knows that he's dropping bricks?

JILL: Well, he says, 'Oh, I've dropped the most frightful bricks,' and 'Oh, I'm dreadful, darling. Take no notice of me.' But he's absolutely marvellous, really, because he gives you enormous confidence, and, if he cares about you, he shows it.

RUSSELL: How did he describe your face?

JILL: 'Strange. The one with the strange face.'

RUSSELL: And you went back and cried a lot, did you?

JILL: I used to cry a great deal then. Yes. That's why my face was so swollen, of course.

RUSSELL: That's why you were fatter in those days?

JILL: Very fat, and full of tears, yes.

RUSSELL: Your life in your little bedroom seems very odd . . .

JILL: It isn't odd at all, it's divine.

RUSSELL: It's odd for the rest of us who have to queue up at Tesco and rush about on buses and things.

JILL: I go and do things like that too.

RUSSELL: You have also said that if you were to end your life, you'd like to do it very majestically.

JILL: Well, yes, I have a terrible fear of old age and I said I'd go and walk out . . . to Malibu beach into the sea, except I hoped it wouldn't be too long because I'd get tired. I'd wear a nice swimsuit and have my hair done. But the thing that really upset me – because it was an interview with Roderick Mann – he said, 'But you'd have to fly there first.' I thought, 'Oh, God I can't bear flying. I might die of a heart attack on the aeroplane and what a waste!' So I think I'll probably go to Southend, or somewhere.

RUSSELL: Or Clacton.

JILL: Yes, lovely, and have some jellied eels and cockles and winkles.

RUSSELL: Then you'll probably change your mind.

JILL: I'm always changing my mind, so . . .

RUSSELL: I suspect that one of the reasons why you're not so nervous at this moment is because one of the main props, if not the main prop, of your affection and your life, namely your husband, is teetering on the edge of the set, waiting . . .

JILL: Oh, I think he's probably left the studio by now.

91

RUSSELL: Do you think he got bored?

JILL: Not bored – frightened. And his daughter, my step-daughter, sitting in the control room, she makes me very nervous.

RUSSELL: Well let's put all our collected nerves together and give a big welcome, ladies and gentlemen, to the man who made England sit up and listen, and he's Jill's husband – Mr John Osborne.

(*applause; music*)

RUSSELL: You've met each other before, haven't you?

JILL: No. It's lovely to meet him.

RUSSELL: You've read so much about him?

JILL: I've read so much about him and all his wives, yes (*pauses*). That's all right, is it?

RUSSELL: That's all right. Go on, go on.

OSBORNE: Very fluent, I thought. Very . . .

JILL: I think they're very lucky women.

RUSSELL: How do you deal with her nervousness? Is she as nervous as she pretends to be?

OSBORNE: She certainly is, yes. No question about that. Most people don't realise what actors and actresses put themselves through is very hard and very rigorous, and the more easy it looks, the more difficult it is really. And yes, she's extremely nervous now.

RUSSELL: Well, she's doing a great job. Before we sink into a pother of mutual admiration (*Jill Bennett laughs*) . . .

JILL: Well, that doesn't often happen!

RUSSELL: Do you ever row with each other at all?

JILL: Yes.

OSBORNE: Oh yes, absolutely.

RUSSELL: Can you remember the last time you had a good ding-dong?

JILL: Yes, last weekend.

OSBORNE: Last week, I should think.

JILL: And he sulks for weeks afterwards, It's not worth it.

OSBORNE: Well I think men usually –

JILL: Don't put people in pigeon-holes.

OSBORNE: No, but I think, men are inclined to suffer longer. They have sulks, you know.

JILL: Their ego's suffering, nothing else.

OSBORNE: Yes. I think, much more, certainly . . . but whereas . . .

RUSSELL: Shall I just slip quietly away somewhere?

JILL: No, no, please . . . what do you think? Do join us.

RUSSELL: I want to know what the last weekend's row was about.

JILL: Oh God, I was rude to him about . . . silly things . . . ludicrous . . . always coming out of nothing.

RUSSELL: Well the obverse side of that is that you treat one another also with enormous amounts of style from time to time. Unusual kinds of style. I mean you invite each other out to lunch and send cars for each other. Is this a system which you have erected on top of the marriage, or has it sprung out of it?

OSBORNE: It's a sort of mutual respect really. I mean I admire what she does and what she's always done, and we have a professional respect, apart from anything else, and care and tact about one another.

RUSSELL: Mmm.

OSBORNE: It sounds awfully self-congratulatory, but I think it's true.

RUSSELL: Well, so long as it's you that's saying it, it's ot too self-congratulatory, is it? Are you trying to tempt her towrds any of your new writing or new plays?

OSBORNE: Well, I've never felt the urge to do that . . .

JILL: Oh!

OSBORNE: No, if I've ever done anything it's been fair objective and if Jill happened to fit into it, I've been very glad. Soetimes she hasn't been able to, for one reason or another.

RUSSELL: Where did you first meet? When were you fir formally introduced, and when did the light gleam in your . . . seral eyes?

OSBORNE: I first met her years ago, when she was married someone else and then, I saw her in a play on television and thoug she was jolly good, and more or less decided to cast her in a pla of mine called *A Patriot For Me.* Which is really when we got to 1ow one another, six or seven years ago.

RUSSELL: But when did the light in your eyes gleam?

JILL: Oh, not for another year.

OSBORNE: Oh, not for a long time.

RUSSELL: When did you know it would be a marriage of tri minds, with or without impediment?

JILL: I don't think we know that yet. But we're hoping for.

OSBORNE: The impediment's there, but . . .

JILL: A lot of impediments, yes, a bit of truth . . .

RUSSELL: You're very diplomatic, Jill, aren't you? Have yu ever thought of taking up politics at all? I mean, you . . .

OSBORNE: Oh, she'd be frightfully good at it.

JILL: No, I wouldn't, because when I lose my temper, evthing goes out of the . . . window, doesn't it?

OSBORNE: Yes. You'd be a very good diplomat's wife, I think.

JILL: Are . . . are you trying to pass me up onto . . .

(audience laughter)

RUSSELL: At least you could push your Press Secretary out of the way when he or she got, you know, uppity.

JILL: Oh yes, I could do that.

OSBORNE: Oh, she could pull class on anybody, any time.

JILL: Oh, I wish you wouldn't talk about class. It's so common.

(John Osborne laughs)

RUSSELL: We know how Jill works, because of rehearsals and appearing in the evening and everything. What about your work schedule: are you a disciplined writer?

OSBORNE: No. Utterly undisciplined.

JILL: Oh, not quite.

OSBORNE: No, I am really, because I just sit and stare at the books and the ceiling for most of the day and . . .

RUSSELL: and look at the wall.

OSBORNE: That sort of thing, yes. When I first started out and was about fifteen, I thought I was going to be what people thought of as being a writer in those days; you did your 1,000 or 2,000 words a day and then you had lunch and took the spaniels for a walk round the hedgerows . . .

JILL: In your Norfolk jacket.

OSBORNE: . . . in my Norfolk jacket, yes. But that never established itself at all as a system with me. I have about forty-eight weeks of pure hell and then three weeks of pure delight when I set to work on something.

RUSSELL: Well, that's not a bad average, though, is it? There are some people who have fifty-two weeks of pure hell.

JILL: Yes. Absolutely.

OSBORNE: Well I've written over twenty plays in about fifteen years. And films, which have never been produced, mostly.

RUSSELL: Because of lack of finance or interest?

OSBORNE: I've always been paid too much in the first place . . .

JILL: He's never told me that!

(audience laughter)

OSBORNE: The only reason for writing films is for the money, because there's very little pleasure in it otherwise. You just get treated like an office boy.

RUSSELL: On the set even?

OSBORNE: Oh yes. I never bother to go to the set. I never get to that stage.

94

JILL: He's always been given the heave-ho by then.

OSBORNE: That's right. I've got the sack by then, so most of the have never seen the light, apart from *Tom Jones*, which was a sort of success at the time.

RUSSELL: Come on—*sort* of success! It was a huge success at the time.

OSBORNE: Seems a long time ago though.

RUSSELL: There's a quotation here which says that you and England —Osborne and England—are 'an enduring double-act'. Do you remember uttering those words?

OSBORNE: No, *I* certainly didn't, and they were certainly said by somebody else.

RUSSELL: Who?

OSBORNE: I don't know. Some journalist I should think made it up.

RUSSELL: Is it a remark which is offensive to you?

OSBORNE: Not at all. I think the idea of patriotism, as love of one's country, can be perverse, or corrupt, like love of God, or women, or whatever you like. But I don't think it's half a bad thing.

RUSSELL: What's turned your anger with England into a kind of acceptance? Age, is it, do you think?

OSBORNE: I don't think I do accept it. I find it less acceptable than ever before. I never found this country more dislikable than I do now, or the environment less likable or more unpleasant. I used to look forward to coming back here when I was abroad, but I don't particularly now; it seems to me brutalised, and everyone's imagination at a very low level.

RUSSELL: Have you evidence of that?

OSBORNE: Well, I think public imagination has coarsened, and has led to a very materialistic way of thinking. In earlier times in this country there was a feeling of the English genius. It's a sort of awful cliché, but there was such a thing and it's evident in the plays of Shakespeare, or the Book of Common Prayer, or all sorts of English institutions. I think that's gone, largely, and it's going more and more. It's a very brutal and unpleasant sight. Tourism has made almost the entire world squalid, and London, for example, is a very squalid place to live now. I look on myself as a Londoner. I used to think one was a citizen of no mean city, but it certainly is not like that any longer; it's littered with human rubbish: Germans and Japanese and Americans. They may bring a lot of money but I don't really believe in that; I think that's just one of those economic mythologies which people subscribe to, but which really have no basis of any sort truth at all. Where I live now, I've lived mostly for the last fifteen or twenty years. It's no longer a pleasant place to live, because it's littered with people one doesn't particularly want to see.

RUSSELL: You make me a little bit sad. As long as it's not littered with empty new potato tins . . .

JILL: It is, actually, but I do put them in the dustbin.

RUSSELL: And that's sometimes emptied?

JILL: Yes. He's made me tidier than I was.

OSBORNE: Oh, she's frightfully tidy.

JILL: Because you've bullied me so. I usen't to be.

RUSSELL: Well, on that note of high optimism, Jill Bennett, John Osborne, thank you very much.

JILL: Thank you very much.

(*applause*)

JEANETTE CHARLES

RUSSELL: Now all of you have seen her looking like this (*holding up a photograph of 'the Queen' in a Buckingham Palace setting*), but I wonder how many of you have caught a glimpse of her looking like this (*holding up a photograph of Jeanette Charles standing in a bus queue*). It's obviously no fun being photographed everywhere you go, as my next guest has discovered. Ladies and gentlemen, pray be seated to receive Mrs Jeanette Charles.

(*applause*)

I suppose the first question is – I don't know really what to call you, so if I just call you Mrs Charles?

JEANETTE: Oh well, you can call me Jeanette now, of course.

RUSSELL: How embarrassing to you personally is your appearance?

JEANETTE: Well, I don't think I've ever had an embarrassing moment. I've had some very frightening moments.

RUSSELL: Frightening?

JEANETTE: Very frightening indeed, yes. In my younger days when I travelled on the Continent, I have actually had odd moments of being surrounded. And – er – not only surrounded but also – er – touched. Particularly in places like – Italy and that, you see?

(*audience roars with laughter*)

I don't think one is aware of the fact that they not only can't believe you're a 'she', but they also want to feel you to make sure that you're alive . . .

RUSSELL: Right.

JEANETTE: But embarrassing, no. Frightening yes, and er – and rather proud at different times, you know. It's almost like being her shadow, and I think many times I've been an unpaid ambassadress. I won't ask for any payment for it, but this is how I've often felt.

RUSSELL: But if you feel like that, maybe God has paid you. Do you see what I mean by that?

JEANETTE: Well now, this is a very funny thing. You put me in mind of a letter I had from a woman in South Africa who wrote to say that if I looked up a certain book in the library, it could be proven that I was an offspring of the illegitimate side of – er – I think it was George III. Well, to be honest with you I've never done that, because I don't want to be an illegitimate anything. So I've actually left it alone.

RUSSELL: It would be too big a shock to your system, that?

JEANETTE: Well, you see, it would be a shock to all my family.

RUSSELL: Right.

JEANETTE: What I was going to say was, evidently there are, I believe, 103 offspring of George III.

RUSSELL: So maybe we're all related to George III somehow?

JEANETTE: Well, I don't know, but if I am, I suppose it would be rather interesting – if somebody else would do the research for me, you see.

RUSSELL: Well, you've just said you don't want to find out too much about that. You want to preserve . . .

JEANETTE: Well, keep it secret. I mean they could find out for me and obviously it would be a private thing. Yes.

RUSSELL: Right. And it's important that one – a person in your position should preserve some mystique, I think, as well.

JEANETTE: Well, this goes back simply because my mother is Dutch. She was born in Amsterdam, and her people were German and Polish and so on, and it possibly could be proved that I am an offspring, far back.

RUSSELL: Right. Now do you feel, as well as *looking* like the Queen, do you feel invested with any kind of royal aura? Do you feel as though you're elevated in any kind of way?

JEANETTE: No – I give out *some*thing, I'm not sure what it is, and I hope I'm modest in saying this. For instance, a lady came up to me not so long ago. I had been on the David Frost show, just before Christmas, and I was in London shopping. This lady, who was rather old, she was an Australian, she came up to me and she said, 'My dear, I know who you are. I've seen you on television, and it's fantastic. I've spent all the money I've got in coming to London so that I can be here to see Princess Anne get married, and possibly to catch a sight of the Royal Family.' And she had me in tears, she was so sad. I had the feeling too, and I mean this seriously, I had the feeling that that lady was dying inwardly. It might sound rather dramatic, but I have come across a lot of people who've spoken to me who think so much of the Royal Family, it's almost like a disease.

RUSSELL: Have you been to Buckingham Palace yourself?

JEANETTE: Well, I did a rather cunning thing one day. A photographer said to me, 'Now, I would like to get you coming out of the gates of Buckingham Palace.' Well, if the audience don't know, the only way to get past the policeman is actually to sign the visitor's book. So what you do, you go and sign the visitor's book, and then you get the photographer to stand on the other side of the road and photograph you as you come out, which is what he did.

RUSSELL: Did you keep a stiff upper lip?

JEANETTE: Oh, indeed I did. I mean – I was being paid for the job, you see, so I had to do it properly, and it came out marvellously, it really did.

RUSSELL: Good. Were you like the Queen when she was Princess Elizabeth . . . in other words, did you look like Princess Elizabeth?

JEANETTE: Yes. Again, I hope I'm modest in what I'm saying, but I have photos that go back to the time that I was sixteen and from that age the bone structure is – you know, it's amazing, it's absolutely amazing. I mean, any angle you see. I've been abroad many many years. My husband is in the oil business, and throughout those years I've collected different books and pictures, not stackfuls and not roomfuls as do some people, just the odd book, and I can put pictures of myself by the side of Princess Elizabeth as she was then, and really, there's no difference.

RUSSELL: Does your husband walk two paces behind you?

(*audience laughter*)

JEANETTE: Well, not really, you see, being abroad as he has in the Middle East countries, it's usual for the lady to walk behind the *husband*, and we have rather this reversal of roles, except that when I'm in the public eye, I do give him a shove.

(*audience laughter*)

We were in a very good class restaurant, Verrey's – you probably know it – at the top of Regent Street one night about two or three years ago. I had an evening dress on and I suppose I looked rather elegant, I felt it. He went to the cloakroom, and (*laughs*) this man came behind him, and my husband wasn't quite sure for what purpose, you know . . .

(*uproar*)

. . . and anyway, the man came up to him and said, 'Excuse me, but you know – that lady – is – is she the Queen? Now I must ask you this because my wife and I are sitting there, and really we just can't go out without asking you.' And my husband said, 'Well, really, no.' He gets embarrassed at times like that, whereas I enjoy it. I mean, why shouldn't I? No harm done, and to sit in a restaurant you have good service . . .

(*audience laughter*)

Better service than you would normally . . .

RUSSELL: I bet you do. I bet you do. What are you doing after the show?

JEANETTE: No, I'm afraid my husband's probably off abroad tomorrow and I have to go home . . . tonight, anyway.

RUSSELL: Right. Right. Now, you have children as well?

JEANETTE: Yes, I have three.

RUSSELL: When did they rumble the fact – when did they begin to see a similarity between you and a certain person?

JEANETTE: I was really amused because for years when the Queen has given her Christmas broadcast, they would sit there and call out, 'There's Mummy'. They look and look at me, and in fact I'm most interested in watching the Queen myself because – and again I hope I'm being modest in saying this – but I'm very truthful – when I *do* look at her I can see myself.

RUSSELL: Have you ever actually seen her close to?

JEANETTE: Yes, I saw her once very close to indeed.

RUSSELL: Did she see *you*?

JEANETTE: Ah. The last time I said this Jean Rook of the *Daily Express* was rather nasty in her column . . .

RUSSELL: About whom?

JEANETTE: About myself.

RUSSELL: Well, that's a distinction you share in common with a large number of other people.

JEANETTE: Well, the way I look at it is this. I mean I am me. I don't exactly have a mask on, and I'm not an actress so I can't make myself up, and if I do have this distinction of looking like the Queen, then I'm very proud, because I am naturally myself, and I mean naturally, without any artifice.

RUSSELL: Right. Let's just pause there slightly, because there are other things to say.

JEANETTE: Do I have my hair done like this all the time? I've been asked that before.

RUSSELL: Well, no, that's part of the thing, but you do, in fact, dress consciously in a way that suggests . . .

JEANETTE: No, no! I said this to a journalist one day when asked if I consciously dressed like her. My answer to you is no. I have always dressed simply because I am very short, and a short person can't wear frills and flounces. It's not possible. O.K., maybe I buy dresses that will now be better for showing on colour TV, but I don't buy a different style of dress to what I've always been used to.

100

RUSSELL: You see, from the waist upwards, if I may approach you this closely, there is a similarity in dress. I mean the Queen is wont — W-O-N-T — to wear pearls and a simple clasp up there, isn't she?

JEANETTE: Yes. Yes, and how many thousands of women wear pearls?

RUSSELL: But how many thousands of women look like the Queen *and* wear pearls?

(*audience laughter*)

JEANETTE: But you see as I said to you before, I am naturally myself.

RUSSELL: Right. O.K. Fine. In a kind of way, therefore, you have been able to turn this accident of birth on your part to your own advantage, lately.

JEANETTE: No. Let's put it like this. There are a lot of people who have made a lot of money out of me. They've photographed me, they have written about me, and they have come to my home, and I've not made a penny out of this.

RUSSELL: But . . . what about the advertisements?

JEANETTE: Yes. People came to me and I suddenly thought to myself, 'Now, if *they* can get money by photographing me, why shouldn't I get a little bit of it myself?' And two model agencies had already approached me, so I approached one that I'd heard was most interesting, and, they were very pleased indeed. So I now do modelling.

RUSSELL: And that doesn't worry you at all? The morality of that doesn't worry you?

JEANETTE: Well, have I done anything wrong? I mean, look, I'm sitting in a chair. I mean, what have I . . .

RUSSELL: No — I'm asking *you* the question. You don't consider that there's anything marginally immoral about that?

JEANETTE: No. What I consider marginally immoral is the fact that there is a French actress who . . . and I think it's because I refused several offers from France to go over there. . . . They would have signed an open cheque if I would just be escorted round Paris or different parts of France, obviously impersonating the Queen and doing and going where they wanted me to. I turned them down flat. Now, about six months after I had done that — and remember I had two or three offers, not only from France but from other countries — after so doing, I did read that a French actress had had the gall to come over and be photographed walking through Harrods.

RUSSELL: I think you speak beautifully at times.

JEANETTE: Thank you very much.

RUSSELL: 'A French actress has the gall' is a marvellous . . .

JEANETTE: Yes.

RUSSELL: You've got the gift of the royal tongue as well. Now, if the Reds who are under our beds, i.e. Communists, emerge from under our beds and begin to attack our vital institutions like our monarchy, that will jeopardise, to a certain extent, your position?

JEANETTE: No, the only thing that would jeopardise my position would be if the Queen abdicated, and I hope for goodness' sake she doesn't do that for quite a few years. As far as the monarchy's concerned I'm a great Royalist myself. Now, I'm sure I will be under attack. I'm sure I will. This is bound to happen, but I read of an Indian who had made a bed for Princess Anne. He came over, and his greatest desire was to see the Queen and the Royalty, and the next thing I read was that he'd been shipped back. I felt very sad about that, and I can assure you that if I had met that man, I would have made his day a little happier. The reason I say this is because, for one instance, a lady in the supermarket came over to me with two little children, and she said, 'I'm sure you're Mrs Charles. You're so like the Queen but I'm sure the Queen wouldn't shop here. But you're not, are you?' And I said, 'Well, no, I'm not.' She said, 'Well, will you do me a great favour? Would you please just talk to my children?' So I went over to them (I think one was about eight and one was about five) and I shook their hands, you know, and I spoke to them and said something about Christmas. I don't remember what it was, and I walked away quickly. Now, if I'm doing anything wrong, then I will keep on doing it, because I remember for instance, when I heard that there was no Father Christmas I got a terrible shock. Now if these children thought they saw the Queen, and I had, in some way, indicated to them they had not seen the Queen, their day would have been spoiled.

RUSSELL: But supposing they go through their lives telling people . . .

JEANETTE: But it doesn't matter you see, because if I look so much like the Queen, it's not important. As far as they're concerned, when they were little children, they *met* the Queen, and it means a lot to little children.

RUSSELL: Do you ever dream of the Queen?

JEANETTE: No. I'll be honest – never. I'm not a Walter Mitty character. I don't go round hoping to be the Queen because you see, I have a husband who has a good position, and there's nothing I want. I have everything in the world I want. I have a good home, in fact I've been very fortunate in my life because I've never actually had to work hard for anything. When I married my husband we had our own home. You know, I've never had any hardship in life.

RUSSELL: Do you have a tiara?

JEANETTE (*laughing*): No. No, I don't. I don't think I'd like to do that kind of dressing up. I mean even in modelling they've never asked me yet. And that *is* impersonation.

RUSSELL: And you wouldn't go that far?

JEANETTE: Well, I don't say I wouldn't go that far . . .

(*audience laughter*)

because – I mean it depends for what reason, you see. If somebody asked me to sit in a chair and actually impersonate the Queen for that picture to be put in a magazine, I would say no. But if it was a family thing, and it was a bit of fun, and they wanted me to sit with a tiara, O.K., maybe I would. But to be honest I've never touched a tiara in my life, so I don't know, really.

RUSSELL: You wouldn't know what to do with it if you found it?

JEANETTE: Well, I'd look darned silly, I mean, walking round with a tiara, wouldn't I?

RUSSELL: In Tesco's you would, yes.

(*audience laughter*)

JEANETTE: Well, not only in Tesco's. In a restaurant. You've got to go to a dressy occasion to have a tiara, and I don't go to that kind of occasion.

RUSSELL: Now, do you realise what an awkward dilemma you've placed me in tonight?

JEANETTE: No – not really. Not unless you tell me.

RUSSELL: Well, every restaurant I go to now, I shall be looking for somebody. And supposing by a strange accident I go to a restaurant which the Queen is dining in and bounce over to her and say, 'Hi, how are you?' and say, 'Haven't I seen you somewhere?'

JEANETTE: I've had that said to me before too. Somebody came up to me – an old couple – one day. They were very sweet, and they were very gracious and they really did think it was she, and they said: 'We're awfully embarrassed at stopping you' – kind of looking round to see if there were any security guards and so on – 'but we do love you.' And I thought that was very, very sweet indeed.

RUSSELL: Well, may I say to you, *you* are obviously a sweet person, you're obviously intensely loyal . . . and . . .

JEANETTE: Well, thank you very much. I am indeed, very loyal, yes.

RUSSELL: Will you do me a favour? Would you do *me* a favour?

JEANETTE: What's that?

RUSSELL: When I'm a hundred, will you send me a telegram?
(*audience laughter*)
JEANETTE: My God, you're younger than I am! I hope I live that long. Thank you very much indeed for inviting me.
RUSSELL: Jeanette Charles, thank you very much. Thank you very much.
(*applause*)

DAME SYBIL THORNDIKE

RUSSELL: It has been said of my last guest tonight, that the only way that she can convey old age is by acting it. The whole of London's theatreland celebrated with her on her ninetieth birthday last year, to mark her lifetime's devotion to the theatre. Ladies and gentlemen, I'm very proud and delighted to welcome to the programme Dame Sybil Thorndike.

(*music; applause*)

All your life, you've championed the causes of various under-dogs, haven't you? I mean, you've fought for a lot of causes?

DAME SYBIL: Oh I have, I've been in lots of causes.

RUSSELL: And a lot of the things you've fought for, like the Trades Union cause and Women's Lib, have all been championed.

DAME SYBIL: They've all done well. I was in the early suffragettes, you see. I didn't go and fight myself, because I was working, but I championed them and spoke at their meetings.

RUSSELL: You didn't chain yourself to any railings, or anything?

DAME SYBIL: I didn't do any of those violent things. I hate violence. I hate violence more than I can say. And I'm sure it's wrong and I don't think it's the way to get things. I think we would have got the vote if we'd just gone on plodding, instead of being so outrageous.

RUSSELL: Right. Now then, if all the causes that you've worked for have been championed, what is there left to fight for now? What are you fighting for now?

DAME SYBIL: Or Lord! What *am* I fighting for now? How to keep alive, I think.

RUSSELL: Yes, but I mean if there were a cause that you could go out and shout for, and talk about and urge on, who would it be? Would you champion Ted Heath?

DAME SYBIL: No. I'm a Socialist, you see. I like Ted Heath very much as a person, I think he's fine, but I'm a Socialist. If I hadn't been a Socialist my husband would never have married me.

RUSSELL: Did you turn for him?

105

DAME SYBIL: Oh yes, I knew when I met him that if I didn't turn Socialist I'd not have a look-in.

RUSSELL: And you were smart enough to do that.

DAME SYBIL: I was smart enough to do that.

RUSSELL: Were there any other girls in the running for him?

DAME SYBIL: Not actually, I think. We were all working too hard to think about that sort of thing. We were all working very hard in repertory in Manchester.

RUSSELL: Where did you meet Lewis?

DAME SYBIL: I met Lewis in the Dublin Zoo. That's where I first spoke to him. He was trying to mesmerise a lioness . . .

(*audience laughter*)

. . . trying to send it to sleep, and he had.

RUSSELL: He had?!

DAME SYBIL: And I thought, 'Well, that's an odd thing to do. He's a nice man.' But I had seen him before on the stage, and I thought, 'I like that man, I like the way he speaks.' And I said to the man sitting next to me, 'Oh, I like the way that man speaks,' and he said, 'But he's not speaking English, he's speaking Welsh.' 'Well,' I said, 'I like Welsh . . . Very quick Welsh.'

RUSSELL: Did he ever mesmerise you?

DAME SYBIL: Mesmerise me? Well, I suppose he *did* . . .

RUSSELL: Or did he ever send you to sleep? Were you ever bored by him?

DAME SYBIL: Never. We fought too much to be bored with each other. Oh, the roof would go off with arguments. Oooh, we argued till we couldn't see out of our eyes.

RUSSELL: What did you argue about?

DAME SYBIL: Everything. Religion, politics . . . though we were both on the same side in both of them. But we argued — we argued the line of every play I was in. Argued the interpretation of plays. Oh, he used to make me mad. I used to spout out something I thought was so good, and he said, 'Oh dear, that's awful.' So we'd go over and over again, because he had a very, very quick ear, the quickest, most musical ear that I've ever met for speech.

RUSSELL: Did you ever have silences? I mean did you ever sulk with each other?

DAME SYBIL: Sulk? That's one thing we *never* did. I don't think he could have ever sulked, and I don't think I could.

RUSSELL: Well then, how did you bring your arguments to an end?

DAME SYBIL: Oh, generally flare up. I'd cry or . . .

RUSSELL: Stamp about?

106

DAME SYBIL: Or stamp about, yes. And we'd say, 'Oh, aren't we fools?'

RUSSELL: And have a quick drink?

DAME SYBIL: Not always — we weren't great drinkers, you know.

RUSSELL: No, I wasn't suggesting . . .

(*audience laughter*)

. . . I was suggesting that you had a celebratory drink, not that you all got sloshed at the end of the day.

DAME SYBIL: No. No. Because we weren't sloshers.

RUSSELL: Right. Now, we heard that during the war, Hitler had got you on a short list.

DAME SYBIL: Wasn't I pleased to hear it!

(*audience laughter*)

Oooh, wasn't it wonderful? But I didn't hear it until afterwards, which was a pity.

RUSSELL: Who told you?

DAME SYBIL: I forget who told me, it was somebody like — Lord Nugent, I think, told me I was on . . .

RUSSELL: And what were you on the list for?

DAME SYBIL: I don't know. Because I was so anti-war and I was a Socialist. A very hot Socialist, and I was all the things that Hitler didn't like.

RUSSELL: You have been a great traveller, haven't you?

DAME SYBIL: Not a great traveller, but I've travelled round the world twice, and never had to pay a penny for it.

RUSSELL: Did you hitch lifts?

DAME SYBIL: No. Always working. I've been round the world twice playing — the whole way round.

RUSSELL: And you're a great walker, or have been a great walker.

DAME SYBIL: Oh, tremendous walker. That's what's done me in now, I think. Miserable — awful to feel that I can't go long walks any more.

RUSSELL: You used to take a long walk every day?

DAME SYBIL: Well, not deliberately, but we used to take our holidays walking. We walked in the mountains in Wales; we walked in France; we walked all over the place. Up in the Lakes. All over the place. All our children are the same. All walkers.

RUSSELL: If you could take a walk tonight, or tomorrow morning with Lewis again, where would you choose to be?

DAME SYBIL: I would go up Snowdon.

RUSSELL: Now, do you believe in God at all?

DAME SYBIL: Of course I believe in God.

RUSSELL: Has your belief got stronger as you've got older?

DAME SYBIL: Yes, stronger, but less — less doctrinal somehow. I don't swallow everything I'm told in church. I go to church regularly and I've got a very fine vicar who is very forward, luckily — otherwise I should get up and argue, I'm sure.

RUSSELL: What do you mean, 'he's very forward'?

DAME SYBIL: Well, he's very forward-thinking.

RUSSELL: Right.

DAME SYBIL: He's very wise and very — er — modern.

RUSSELL: Does he mind that you've got more questioning in your beliefs than you were some time ago?

DAME SYBIL: No — nobody minds, because I've always questioned. My father was a parson, you see, and he brought us up to argue. We used to argue the toss when we came home from Sunday church, and father had been preaching. We pulled his sermon to bits at lunch.

RUSSELL: That wasn't a very kind family thing . . .

DAME SYBIL: Oh yes, it was wonderful. We lived on arguments. Oh, I couldn't do without a good old argument. I think it would be dreadful to be married to anybody who said, 'Yes, dear', or 'No, dear'. Wouldn't it be awful? Oh, I'd kill them.

RUSSELL: Now you've said what you like to very important people, haven't you? I mean, you said a few mouthfuls to the Duke of Edinburgh not long ago.

DAME SYBIL: Wasn't it awful?

RUSSELL: Tell us about that.

DAME SYBIL: Well, the Duke of Edinburgh was giving — what do they call it? — an oration in Westminster Abbey, and I always go to the orations because I go to everything that I can in Westminster Abbey because I love it very much . . . love it as a centre. And I knew he was going to speak. He gave the most wonderful forty-minute address. It might have been — well, it might have been a Socialist speaking. And then I went into the garden afterwards, and met him. But I didn't meet him properly. I saw him about the place and I said 'Oh, I think you're wonderful.' I never said 'Your Highness' or 'Your . . .' — whatever you do call him . . .

(*audience laughter*)

. . . And I said, 'I think you're wonderful. Did you write that all yourself?' And he said, 'Yes, I did.' I said, 'Well, I think it's marvellous.' Then I said an awful thing. I said, 'I never would have thought a member of the Royal Family would have done such a thing.'

(*audience laughter*)

Wasn't it wonderful? Oh, but it was fine.

RUSSELL: And what did he say to you then?

DAME SYBIL: Oh, he just laughed. Oh, I felt so ashamed. You know when you feel a thing you don't think, you just go slap ahead and . . . say exactly what you think, don't you?

RUSSELL: He didn't ask for your Damehood back again, did he?

DAME SYBIL: No he didn't, but I rather wonder he didn't.

RUSSELL: Now, let's talk a bit about the theatre.

DAME SYBIL: Yes.

RUSSELL: Looking back over ninety years, what has been the most memorable moment in the theatre for you?

DAME SYBIL: Do you mean personally?

RUSSELL: Personally, privately memorable.

DAME SYBIL: The first night of *Saint Joan* was the most wonderful experience I've ever had, and also, there was one other wonderful one when I played *The Trojan Women* first for the inauguration of the League of Nations Union. That was absolutely thrilling.

RUSSELL: But *Saint Joan* sticks out ahead?

DAME SYBIL: *Saint Joan* sticks out ahead because it was exactly what I wanted to say.

RUSSELL: Were you not paralysed with nerves – you as the first-ever Saint Joan?

DAME SYBIL: I'm always paralysed with nerves on a First Night, but *Saint Joan* was the only time I've not been nervous. Isn't it extraordinary? The moment I heard those trumpets, I was exalted.

RUSSELL: Was George Bernard Shaw there?

DAME SYBIL: Oh, of course he was.

RUSSELL: What did he have to say about it?

DAME SYBIL: Ooh, he didn't – afterwards. Oh, . . . he was all right. (*audience laughter*)

Oh, I never had such . . . and I got better you know, I wasn't at the top on the First Night.

RUSSELL: How old were you then?

DAME SYBIL: Forty-two! And I was playing a girl of nineteen. But you see, a girl of nineteen in those days was much older.

RUSSELL: Right . . .

DAME SYBIL: It's silly to make Joan a little, sweet person. She wasn't. She was tough, and not so young neither. Oh, she was young when she first heard her voices – she was only fourteen when she first heard voices.

RUSSELL: Was Shaw ever rude to you? Because he has an enormous reputation for being scabrous and vitriolic . . .

DAME SYBIL: I cannot think how he got that name. He could be vitriolic on the platform, but in real life, and if you heard him at rehearsal, I don't think he ever said a thing which made anybody feel uncomfortable. In fact, one not very good actor said, 'Do you know, Mr Shaw makes me feel as if I'm a very good actor.' I said, 'Well, that's fine.' He had a way of putting things that made you feel – 'Oh, I'm all right.'

RUSSELL: Even though you may not have been terribly good?

DAME SYBIL: Even though you may not have been terribly good.

RUSSELL: Now, those are the days in the theatre. You don't go to the theatre as much now – and you don't act as much now. What do you do to occupy your time in other ways? Do you watch the box?

DAME SYBIL: Oh, I do. I watch it tremendously. But I don't like it like the theatre. Don't you think I do.

RUSSELL: Oh no.

DAME SYBIL: Oh no, I miss the theatre awfully. I do go to the theatre sometimes, but I'm finding it difficult to hear.

RUSSELL: What about watching television? What are your favourite programmes?

DAME SYBIL: My favourite programme? *Basil Brush*.

(*audience laughter and applause*)

Oh, I simply love him, and . . .

RUSSELL: Why do you like Basil Brush?

DAME SYBIL: Oh, because he's so awful. That terrible laugh, and I'm afraid I get like him sometimes, and I find myself going 'ha ha ha ha'!

RUSSELL: What else do you like?

DAME SYBIL: Oh, I like – what's that lovely one that's been on lately – just come off? – *Upstairs, Downstairs*.

(*audience applause and agreement*)

I love the sentimental ones.

RUSSELL: You do. Do you ever cry when you're watching?

DAME SYBIL: Ooh yes, and somehow or other because it's in a photograph, it's realler than it is in the theatre to me, because the theatre's always larger size to me, and I know the tricks.

RUSSELL: Well now, we're here in a kind of performance attitude, and you're not going to the theatre as often as you did. I would like you, if you would, to perform privately for us now . . .

DAME SYBIL: What?

RUSSELL: A little poetry. Some little poetry, because your voice is gorgeous to listen to . . .

DAME SYBIL: Is it?

RUSSELL: It's like warm velvet washing over me.

DAME SYBIL: Oh, Lord!

RUSSELL: Is there anything up — is there anything up your sleeve — anything medieval?

DAME SYBIL: Yes. I don't read a great deal of modern poetry because I can't understand what they're talking about . . . That's the *very* moderns. I like some of the ancient moderns, like Cecil Spring Rice . . . Yes — and the other boy, Cecil Day Lewis. I love him. I love a lot of them, but I like the old boys . . .

RUSSELL: What about 'Nothing is to man so dear . . .'?

DAME SYBIL: Oh, do you know that poem?

RUSSELL: Yes, I do.

DAME SYBIL: Well, that's 1300 . . .

RUSSELL: That's a long way back.

DAME SYBIL: And it's just as obscure as some of the poems are nowadays. But it's a lovely poem. Shall I say it?

RUSSELL: Yes. Yes.

DAME SYBIL: It's 'Wommanys Love'.

> *No thyng is to man so dere*
> *As wommanys love in gode manere.*
> *A gode womman is mannys blys,*
> *There here love right and stedfast is.*
> *There is no solas under hevene,*
> *Of alle that a man may nevene,*
> *That shuld a man do so moche glew*
> *As a gode womman that loveth trew.*
> *Ne derer is none in Goddys hurde*
> *Than a chaste womman with lovely worde.*

(*applause*)

DAME SYBIL: Such ridiculous words.

RUSSELL: It doesn't matter. You do it magnificently. Dame Sybil, thank you very much indeed.

DAME SYBIL: Thank you.

(*applause*)

111

FREDDIE TRUEMAN

RUSSELL: What can I say about my next guest that you don't already know? Ladies, and gentlemen, the man who once sat next to the Prime Minister of India at lunch and said 'Pass the salt, Gunga Din', Mr Freddie Trueman.

(*applause; music*)

You're known as 'Fiery Fred', aren't you, from time to time? Is that a term of affection, or are people angry with you at times?

TRUEMAN: I've never bothered to find out, Russell. I couldn't care less what they call me as long as they spell my name right. I don't want somebody else getting the fame.

(*audience laughter*)

RUSSELL: You said something amazingly funny about a sheik once, do you remember that?

TRUEMAN: Oh, that story's true, yes. I thought everyone had forgotten about it, but John Arlott in the book *Fred: Portrait of a Fast Bowler* dug that one up. We were on the way to Australia. I think it was '62/'63 trip, and at that time we were playing either . . . I think it was either 85 overs and 200 or 200 runs, whichever were the sooner and you got a new ball. The captain could call in the new ball. And I was stood there having a drink one night, a bit fed up at one of these government cocktail parties, and this sheik arrived and somebody said: 'See the fellow there, Fred? He's got 198 wives.' I said: 'Yes, if he gets another two he can have a new ball.'

(*audience laughter*)

RUSSELL (*primly*): Well, thank you very much, Freddie. Are there plenty more where that came from?

TRUEMAN: Oh, there's a lot more, yes.

RUSSELL: We could go on all night, could we? Let's get back to you though, and talk about you personally. In all this sort of jet-setting that eventually overtook you when you became a famous cricketer, how easy was it for you to keep your social end up? You said that you got bored from time to time at these parties . . .

TRUEMAN: When I went down to Australia I used to get fed up of them saying, 'What do you think of our beer? What do you think of our beaches? What do you think of our women? What do you think of our hotels?' You know. And one night I was somewhere . . . I forget where . . . some government cocktail party again. I'd been invited —you know, they hadn't found out about me then . . .

(*audience laughter*)

Some naval commander said to me, 'What do you think to our bridge?' And I was fed up with it, I'd had it for five months and I just said, 'I'll tell you something about your bridge, shall I?' I said, 'That bridge was built by a firm called Dorman-Long of Middlesbrough, Yorkshire, my county. You changed the currency half-way through the building of it. It lost them half a million quid and, what's more, you're still charging two bob a time to get over and you haven't paid for it yet.'

(*audience laughter*)

RUSSELL: You had a very close relationship with your Dad, didn't you?

TRUEMAN: Oh yes, very close with the old man, yes. He was —in his own way and in his own class —he was a very, very fine cricketer. He had four sons of which I was one, and I always believed that my eldest brother and my youngest brother should definitely have played in first-class county cricket, because they were good enough. But they didn't seem to want to take it up. One took to betting horses and gambling and worked down the pit. He was quite happy, so fair enough —a man's happy in his environment, leave him alone. The other brother didn't want to follow me because I'd been fairly successful and he did time in the R.A.F.

RUSSELL: Was your Dad proud of you?

TRUEMAN: Oh, yes. Immensely proud. You know . . . the old man, he's passed on now, bless his heart, but, I remember getting my cap for Yorkshire. I think we were playing against Essex at Bradford about 1950–51 time, on the Monday evening, and I got my cap for my county. If you got a cap with Yorkshire in 1950, it was worth 25 quid a week at least in the leagues, you know, and let's face it, times were a bit different than they are now, and 25 quid was a lot of money . . .

RUSSELL: Absolutely.

TRUEMAN: And he was on the night shift at the colliery, I remember that. And in those days I couldn't drive a car. I couldn't afford one anyway. I used to travel by train, and I got home after the match about twenty to eleven and he was sat in the chair. He said to me,

113

'Where is it?' And I said, 'Where's what?' And he said, 'Come on, where is it?' and I said, 'Where's what?' You know, I was kidding him along. And he said, 'Your cap.' And I said, 'What cap?' He said, 'Come on, your Yorkshire cap. Where is it?' And he'd had the night off work, he hadn't gone to work, you see. 'Course, this is a Yorkshireman's life – his son, capped for Yorkshire, means everything, you see. To hell with England, Yorkshire will do, you know, and I gave him my cap.

RUSSELL: And when he died . . .

TRUEMAN: Oh, when he died, yes, we put the cap in his coffin, yes, and he took it to his grave.

RUSSELL: Now, when you were working and when you were at the height of your prowess as a cricketer, did you work better, do you think, when you had two or three pints inside you?

TRUEMAN: Well that, now that's another bit of a fallacy, you see. O.K., I'm like a lot more people, like a lot of these people sat in this audience tonight. They've been at work all day, and if they want a pint of beer at night what's wrong with that? What's wrong in drinking a pint or two of beer? I've no time for the person who tries to drink twenty-five, thirty pints Friday night, Saturday night and skint on Tuesday, you know. I've no time for them at all. A person can enjoy a pint of beer without getting a bath in it.

(*audience laughter*)

I do on occasions enjoy a pint of beer. But right throughout my cricketing career, and even through my life, nobody can ever say that they saw Freddie Trueman inebriated, or in a drunken state, because I've never been that way, *would* never be that way.

RUSSELL: But it did help to lubricate a bit?

TRUEMAN: I would reckon that when I bowled like I did bowl, and don't forget in my time that I had to do a hell of a lot more bowling than they do now. You know I sit and laugh when I see bowlers saying they're tired when they've bowled five hundred overs. You know, I'm forty-three, I could bowl five hundred overs their pace with my left arm still, and I wouldn't be tired.

(*audience laughter*)

RUSSELL: Well, what do you take – pills? Or what do you do?

TRUEMAN: No, it's easy. I mean, if you've got a rhythmical run-up and you've got an action and you're balanced, it's easy . . . It becomes hard work when you haven't got these things, and you're trying to be something that you haven't got the equipment for.

RUSSELL: You've got very trendy hair, haven't you, these days?

114

TRUEMAN: Yes – when it's cut, it's even better . . .

(*audience laughter*)

No, but getting back, you know, I used to bowl thirty overs in a day at my pace, which is a hell of a lot quicker than some of them are today. Well, *any* of them are today anyway. Let's face it, Russell, look at cricket today. To me it's still the greatest game in the world. I was a cricketer, a professional cricketer, but, you know, they play a week, they have a week off. In fact, when you look at the fixture list in April you can book your holidays.

(*audience laughter*)

I used to play thirty-eight matches a year, six days a week.

RUSSELL: Do I take it that you don't like one-day cricket?

TRUEMAN: Not particularly. I think it takes away the . . . art of the game. I think what happens is that we get people, bowlers especially, producing false figures and living on it. You come to the last seven or eight overs and a bowler's bowling: all he's got to do if he's got any sense is stick it right in the block-hole. Where the hell can he hit it? He can't hit it anywhere . . . unless he has a lot of luck. He's got to try to stop it, and so people are hitting across the line of the bowl and what happens? Somebody finishes up – did not bowl badly to start with, probably, got 1 for 10, somebody's had a swing at them in the last eight overs and they finish with 5 for 22.

RUSSELL: So you think it's getting more exciting?

TRUEMAN: But of course it's getting more exciting, it's bringing people into the ground, which is what it's all about, bringing crowds in – revenue.

RUSSELL: You've been talking just now about people being tired now but wouldn't have been in your day, or *you* wouldn't have been tired. Isn't that part of the rosy retrospective glow that you see through rosy spectacles as you look back at your career and what things were like?

TRUEMAN: No.

RUSSELL: You don't?

TRUEMAN: Because there's one thing we're certain. No matter how long they've played, they've never enjoyed the game of cricket as much as I enjoyed it. Never.

RUSSELL: You had a real good time.

TRUEMAN: Oh yes. Every time I walked on to a cricket field I felt nine foot six, and about four foot wide.

(*audience laughter*)

Every time I walked on to a cricket field I felt – the tops.

RUSSELL: It's a pity we can't see you walk on a cricket field again.
TRUEMAN: Well I don't know about that, I don't know about that.
RUSSELL: Do people ever tempt you with any kind of offers?
TRUEMAN: Well, for two overs I could blind them, you know. But I don't know what would happen for the rest of the day.
(*audience laughter*)
RUSSELL: Well, if you ever do, you can come back and tell us all about it. Fred Trueman, thank you very much indeed.
TRUEMAN: Thank you very much indeed.
(*applause*)

JUNE HAVOC

Excerpt from Elia Kazan's Gentlemen's Agreement, *starring Gregory Peck, Dorothy McGuire and June Havoc.*

RUSSELL: Ladies and gentlemen, Miss June Havoc!

(*applause; music*)

Dare you tell us what year that was made in?

JUNE: I dare, if only I could remember. Let's see now, I'm 110 years old today, that was . . . I don't remember, but it was in the late 'forties, all right? We all looked so young and hungry.

RUSSELL: Everything's trim and white, and Mr Peck's hair is all short . . .

JUNE: We were lean-looking then, weren't we? Well, that's a long time ago, and there's a whole new world: forty films later, and a lot of water under the bridge (*laughs*). Oh I shouldn't say that—that's very rude, no.

RUSSELL: You're doing fine. Now, let's talk about the later bits first.

JUNE: I direct. I direct a great deal now. For the last fifteen or sixteen years I have been mostly directing and writing. I have written a play, which was done in New York, on Broadway. And now I have written a new one which is going to be done next season in Minneapolis.

RUSSELL: And you sit down and cull it out from the clouds, and write it?

JUNE: Oh no, I sit down in total agony. Writing is just the loneliest, saddest, most . . . oh, but not as bad as acting, because acting is really the curse of the world. Oh God, it's terrifying being an actor! I'm so glad I don't have to act any more—I get frightened at the thought of it!

RUSSELL: Were you frightened all the time you were doing it?

JUNE: All the time.

RUSSELL: Why did you do it?

JUNE: Because I loved it . . .

(*audience laughter*)

It is like being in love with a fickle man . . . who is too attractive to let go, in spite of what he does to you!

(*laughter from a lady*)

117

Some woman understands! (*laughs*)

RUSSELL: Is it tough doing all the things that you now do? Isn't it a kind of tough, commercial, hard, difficult, abrasive world that you are living in?

JUNE: Oh but it can't be! I am a theatre life. I have never known anything else. Let's see now. Up until the age of two I didn't do anything, I just sat around, eating up the profits.

(*audience laughter*)

But I have been working ever since. And since two, I have worked in the world and among the people whom I adore and understand. I have been in the theatre all my life. I've been very lucky.

RUSSELL: Now people tell us these days that in America the theatre is in trouble. There are constant cries that the theatre is in trouble.

JUNE: Yes, that's true.

RUSSELL: Now, is it not tough for you to make a commercial go in that area?

JUNE: Yes, it is. It is very tough — I think that's one of the reasons why I write, and why I direct, and why I do so many things. About ten years ago, I looked at myself and I said, 'My dear, you're not going to mature gracefully unless you stop doing all these silly things for money.' You know? '. . . Which are causing migraine headaches . . .' and I'd got an ulcer from it, and I'm not going to lie in a corner and die of bleeding, because of some role that I hate myself in and doing forty films and how many am I proud of? I'd say maybe three out of forty — that's not a good average. So, if you don't want to watch yourself doing a commercial — and I just don't want to watch myself doing a commercial . . . Well, that's the new world, and I don't want me in that world. So I said, 'No', and I turned my back on it, and I've been making a good life for myself, doing the things I wanted to do. So I'm only lucky.

RUSSELL: How clever have you had to be in the new life that you are making? That is to say, have you traded on your femininity, or have you put to use all the political things . . .

JUNE: You go too far!

RUSSELL: I haven't started yet.

(*audience laughter*)

JUNE: Oh my dear, I've heard you're very rough, particularly on women! Well, it's a man's world in which I find myself, and it's quite true, men did open the doors — but it's very useless because they're standing blocking the entrance.

(*audience laughter*)

118

So it doesn't help an awful lot. It reminds me of an experience I had here in London. I was doing a large special on the BBC. and I was lying in this lovely bed. It was a wonderful Somerset Maugham thing — I don't know if anybody remembers it. But I was over there with one of those attractive Edwardian men, and I was under what we call at home a comforter, which you call an eiderdown. And I said, 'This comforter is very warm,' which got a nice big laugh. And then I said, 'Please, I just want to ask one thing before we take the shot — could I please have one little light over there?' And this wonderful voice of the director came out — he's invisible, of course — and said, 'Miss Havoc, you seem to forget — we British invented television.' So I said, 'Yes, I know you did, but you didn't invent women. Could I have a light over there?'

(*audience laughter*)

He gave it to me! So you see — it does take a few wiles.

RUSSELL: You wrote, about ten or twelve years ago, a book called *Early Havoc* in which you describe your early days.

JUNE: Yes, up to fourteen.

RUSSELL: Right. Including an extraordinary episode as a competitor in marathon dances. We know very little of that here, though a lot of us have seen the film called *They Shoot Horses, Don't They?* But you were actually a part of that scene, weren't you?

JUNE: I was in seven dance marathons from the time I was thirteen to about fifteen. You see, with the great American Depression, which h dly anyone has ever been very interested in, and rightfully so (*laughs*), everybody kept it a secret: all one knew about the country was that it was on its knees. In the Middle West, where the crops had failed, it just seemed that the thumb of disaster was on the entire country. There was no money. People were jumping out of buildings, people were standing on corners — distinguished men — doctors, lawyers with rags wrapped on their feet, selling apples which no one bought. But people were literally hungry. I was thirteen years old and I was among the hungry. And I had been a great big vaudeville star, and I had had a beautiful life, since the age of two, until everything disappeared rapidly when I was around eleven. I got married when I was twelve-and-a-half, and got away from that, thinking that maybe if I got out into this great big world, I might have a chance at the fight. You know, the good fight . . . Well, I got out into the big world, and there was no one to fight — everybody was starving. And there were things called dance marathons.

RUSSELL: Describe them, describe them.

JUNE: Well, for twenty-four hours a day one stood partnered in a group. Once every hour, a bell rang, and you rushed off to rest quarters, and you slept for eleven minutes, out of fifteen – the other minutes were taken in getting to and from the floor. You were on your feet twenty-four hours a day, and then later, after one thousand hours, you went two hours without a break, and then, later, three hours. And then there were sprints, where you ran like a beast, together, and turned at the corners, until somebody fell down. But the thing about it was, that I am in that record book.

RUSSELL: *The Guinness Book of Records.*

JUNE: I'm in that! You must look me up there! I'm in it – I danced thirty-six hundred hours, and I have the record.

RUSSELL: Thirty-six hundred hours sprint?

JUNE: That's four-and-a-half months, yes. That's the one that I won.

RUSSELL: But you don't mean . . . wait a minute, hold on, you don't mean thirty-six hundred hours straight?

JUNE: Oh yes – straight through. In the early part you had eleven minutes out of the hour. And then later on you had eleven minutes out of every two or three hours. And then later on you had none at all – until you dropped. And I was the last to drop, with a very funny man who had very flat feet. And I can't imagine why (*laughs*).

RUSSELL: What did you feel like?

JUNE: Well, it's quite strange, the kind of energy that was in that. You see, the people didn't know they were tragic – that was the sad part of them. I was so young and ignorant and full of beans myself at the time that I didn't realise . . . Everyone thought it was great, funny! They thought they were in the Olympics! They were pathetic, with their pride. You'd think that they were vaudeville stars. They had this great, monstrous pride – 'I will stand up longer than you'll stand up!' My dear, it was absolutely in the food. Well, anyway, they may as well have hit us in the stomach as have given us that food.

RUSSELL: People came to watch?

JUNE: Oh, oh, how they loved it! They loved us, because 'There but for the grace of God go I'. And there was a lot of that identification. You see, it was entertainment to see someone more degraded than yourself during that time. And the dance marathon was about as degraded as a human being could be. And so people brushed their teeth and shaved and did their hair on the floor, because there was no time to go and do anything secretly. You only had that very short time, and everyone was watching: the ladies watched the ladies, the gentleman – I don't want you to get the wrong idea. But it was all, very proper – in fact, terribly proper.

RUSSELL: Well, what do you mean: when people went to the lavatory it was proper?

JUNE: People went, but the same sexes went with you, to be sure that you didn't fall asleep in there and die. You know, because after dancing about two thousand hours, if you weren't picked up every few hours, and put down again when you dropped out, and picked up and put down, and picked up, they discovered, early on, one just slept straight through and died.

RUSSELL: It is horrific, isn't it? The whole thing is.

JUNE: They lost a lot of people that way, and so they stopped doing it.

RUSSELL: When you got to the end of your thirty-six hundred hours, what kind of prizes did you win?

JUNE: Oh, that was amusing. I got a lot of bills, and about $26 and 72 cents at the end of thirty-six hundred hours. The bills said that I had sent out for things like celery, because if you made a cud of celery, it helped you stay awake. I can remember sending off for a little bit – not that much! And you know, you got the bills instead of the prize money. – It was all promoters. It was all run by gangsters, simply because there was an awful lot of money in it. Those men used to make $400,000 on a gate. Now, in 1933 $400,000 was an awful lot of money.

RUSSELL: A hell of a lot of money.

JUNE: Yes. It isn't really worth a lot of our time now, but then it was big money. So the dance marathons formed a large part of my adolescence, and taught me an enormous amount about values. There were people on that floor who had been nice people, who had had good lives, and there were a lot of not young people who were out there on that floor. I was the youngest always, in all seven shows; by far I was the youngest.

RUSSELL: Was your childhood a happy one?

JUNE: Oh, yes.

RUSSELL: While you were on the stage?

JUNE: While I was on the stage, it was sheer joy. I loved my audience and I was lucky – they loved me. No, my whole theatrical life has been quite beautiful.

RUSSELL: And fairly fully recorded (*June Havoc laughs*). I don't necessarily mean by you, but your sister was Gypsy Rose Lee . . .

JUNE: Yes.

RUSSELL: . . . and your mama was . . .

JUNE: Mama was not in theatre.

RUSSELL: No, but she made sure that both of *you* were, didn't she?

JUNE: No . . . I was the first. I was in theatre from the time I was two, until about six, alone. And then, after I was established, I had an act called 'Baby June and her Pals', with a little boy who whistled and danced and sang—and I don't know what's ever happened to him—and then later the act got larger and larger, and there were six little boys. My sister joined when I was about seven. And . . . then we went on and on, and I left when I was twelve-and-a-half because that was the end of vaudeville.

RUSSELL: What prompted you or tempted you to get married when you were twelve?

JUNE: Escape. I guess a lot of kids feel that way—that if they were out on their own, away from parental guidance, they would do better. Well, I hadn't been educated. I wanted something. If ever there was a sketch on the bill with a real actress, oh God! I would follow her around like a puppy dog. The essence of anything legitimate just sent me really wild with joy, and I knew that's what I wanted. But I was in the wrong family for that. And I wanted it so much that I tore away and proposed to this poor, unfortunate child.

RUSSELL: How old was he?

JUNE: I think eighteen, or something like that. I bewitched him, and got him to take me away. We were married in the state of Nebraska, and even if the man *had* looked up and asked me how old I was—which he didn't bother to do—it was twelve years old without parents' consent, in that state. So you see, I would have been safe. I found that out later. But anyway, this child and I ran off to nothingness, and there was nothing to eat. It was starvation, and in the dance marathon they fed you twelve times every twenty-four hours: of course, you had to stand up while you ate it, but at least it was food! —which was better than I had been getting.

RUSSELL: How long did that marriage last?

JUNE: Well, off and on about four years.

RUSSELL: And things have changed a great deal now. The scene is not the same now, I think. We ought to dispel a bit of the gloom that we have been building over ourselves.

JUNE: Yes, I was very lucky. I attracted an extremely magnificent gentleman, and we're having our twenty-fifth wedding anniversary over the Christmas holidays. We're going to shoot off rockets and light up the whole sky. Everybody's invited. Will you all come? Please do.

(audience laughter)

RUSSELL: Well, don't forget there are charter flights now, so don't invite too many people!

(audience laughter; applause)

TONY CURTIS

RUSSELL: He went to Hollywood at the age of twenty-three, with a Tony Curtis haircut and a giant inferiority complex, he matched Hollywood at its own game and became a star and a rich man. Along the way he parted from two wives and a lot of money in his search for security at the hands of numerous psychiatrists. Now he says he's happier than he's ever been before in his life, and he's here to share his secret. Ladies and gentlemen, Tony Curtis.

(*music; applause*)

Is it a real claim, that you're happier now than you've ever been?

CURTIS: Psychiatrists and marriages and all in all, I'm as happy as ever. Like some Hollywood fairy-tale, if you'll excuse the vernacular. I don't feel any tensions of any kind. You know, I find that my attentions are quite concentrated.

RUSSELL: You've had reasonably rough rides earlier on in your life.

CURTIS: Everybody has a rough ride, baby — if you'll excuse the vernacular again. I think everybody does. Each one of us has a wonderful way of feeding ourselves, like a battery that charges itself, in a way. Like taking it from the sun.

RUSSELL: Are you a sun worshipper?

CURTIS: I like the sun very much. I feel that certain energies are revitalised in our system by the sun. I've certain theories about diet and the way we should live, you know. Necessarily, it doesn't have much to do with power cuts, power failures, and not too much petrol around or problems of that nature.

RUSSELL (*laughing*): And no sun around either.

(*audience laughter*)

How much of the happy state that you're in now — the state of ease with nature and things — do you think you owe to the extensive psychiatric treatment that you've gone through?

CURTIS: Absolutely nothing.

(*audience laughter*)

RUSSELL: You've spent a hell of a lot of money on psychiatrists.

CURTIS: Well, *I* didn't. My insurance company did. I wouldn't have

124

gotten it if they didn't pay for it. I needed psychiatry like someone needs someone to talk to. We all have parents, right? Well, some of us are fortunate, we can talk to our parents, and some of us are not. And who do you talk to—a best friend?

I have a friend in California who once told me the definition of a very good friend is someone who is doing slightly worse than you in the same profession. And I thought that was very astute. It really nailed it for me: you know, 'How you doing? Oh, isn't that a shame?' You know . . . that's human nature. Why deny yourself those emotions?

I feel you must seek it in yourself. You must make yourself whole, not use other people as a measuring stick. When I was a kid and started in movies, the big game was: 'How is Paul Newman doing?' or 'How is Marlon Brando doing?' Using each other as mirrors so to speak. And you shouldn't do that. I never did that and I don't do it now.

RUSSELL: Do you consider that you got a fair deal in your early days in Hollywood?

CURTIS: Well, I made it. I mean, that's as fair as you can get for a guy that came out of my background, which was nothing. I had no education. I came from a very poor family—not that being poor means you lack the qualities of an aristocrat. Because we all are aristocrats. We all can be a king or a queen. It's just that we weren't born in that proper crib. Right? So you find yourself born somewhere where no one thinks you're the king. You walk around saying: 'I'm the king.' They say: 'Get out of the house.'

(*audience laughter*)

We all started out that way, and I was very, very fortunate and very privileged that I was able to make a career out of my life.

RUSSELL: Can you remember one instance where you actually closed the door on your poor family background, and opened the Hollywood door?

CURTIS: There wasn't any real dramatic moment, you know, Russell. I just got in the belly of a big iron bird, the TWA constellation, and flew to California and started a seven-year contract in 1948.

RUSSELL: But you couldn't just walk out of the Bronx and opt to catch the airplane.

CURTIS: Well, I was doing a play in New York City. I wanted to be an actor and so I went to a dramatic school. When the war was over in America, veterans were allowed to use the GI Bill of Rights, which meant that you were able to go to a college of your choice and study what you wanted. In my case it was acting.

125

I was lucky in the sense that I had an opportunity for two years not to have to go out and find a proper kind of a job. I was paid so much money – 65 bucks a month, which is what? – about £20 or so a month. But I lived in New York, so that was easy for me.

They paid for the tuiton at the school. So for two years I vamped until I could get started in pictures. And that was my only aim, Russell. That's all I ever wanted to be – a movie actor.

RUSSELL: And when you got into the belly of this iron bird and flew down, did you have great delusions about: 'I'm gonna hit Hollywood sideways. I'm going to be the big man, the big star?'

CURTIS: Well, I had those dreams, those aspirations. I mean, I wasn't going out there to be a failure.

(*audience laughter*)

I really wanted to be big time; I dedicated and drove my life and it had a lot of repercussions. When you become very ambitious; you're willing to eliminate a lot of the niceties, so to speak, and a lot of the subtleties of living. You give up friendships, maybe lasting relationships, at that early period in your life. But to me, everything is like dropping a stone into a pond and seeing the waves. You know, whatever you do today is going to pay you off two-and-a-half weeks from now or a fortnight from now or thirty-seven years from now. Somewhere along the line it comes back to you.

RUSSELL: Well, that's a very dangerous philosophy. Does that mean you have to carefully consider everything that you do?

CURTIS: It means that you should care for absolutely nothing, plan absolutely nothing – just live your life as you wish to live it. Because if you try to plan anything, you're just gonna find yourself . . .

RUSSELL: Screwed up.

CURTIS: 'Screwed up' is right. I think the joy of living is the spontaneity of this moment that you and I are speaking.

RUSSELL: Which prompts me to ask you, off the top of my head: do you fall in love easily?

CURTIS: Every minute I can.

(*audience laughter*)

With anything and anybody, you know. Life should be that way, I feel. If you don't have the freedom of your own mind to express and behave in the way you wish when you get home, then you have nothing.

RUSSELL: When you did the Boston Strangler, did you have any qualms about taking on that part?

CURTIS: Yes, I did, Russell. It was an incredible period of time –

126

1965 in Boston. Boston is very much like London, you know. It's very English, in the sense that the town was locked up. I mean, there was nobody in the streets at night. For about eighteen months the Boston Strangler drove everyone off the streets, because of these incredible, horrendous murders. And the man was a genius, a particular genius in the sense that he could remember anything in any room quickly. He'd come into a room, look around, walk out and be able, twenty minutes, thirty minutes later, to tell you everything he saw. He murdered thirteen women; that's how many he admitted to. There must be many more that he did. He assaulted over a thousand women when he was in the army in Germany. Not only did that take a lot of time, but a lot of vitamins.

(*audience laughter*)

He murdered these thirteen women. Now you try murdering someone. I mean, you're gonna leave some kind of a hint somewhere.

RUSSELL: Right.

CURTIS: One afternoon the door's gonna knock, and a voice will say: 'Come with us.' This man murdered thirteen people and no one ever knew about it. There wasn't anything that related one murder to the next. It was just by accident that three of them were nurses. There was one black girl; there were three white young girls; there were old women, young women. There was never any set pattern. And the only reason they caught Albert de Salvo was because he admitted that he had done these murders.

RUSSELL: Having described all that, luridly, and almost grotesquely, as you have . . .

CURTIS: Oh, thank you.

RUSSELL: . . . what therefore leaned you over to the part?

CURTIS: Well, the sense of this abstractness. You know, unless you're strangled you have no idea of the panic, the fear. Even if you saw it in a movie, you'd just have no idea what it's all like until you live it. And you're just never going to.

RUSSELL: Were you frightened at all while you were doing it?

CURTIS: It took my breath away. The idea of a man that would go ahead and want to destroy women – why would someone want to do that? What drove him to that? So I went to a great deal of study to find out about this person, Albert de Salvo. I studied his background, got all the material that was available: letters that he had written, interviews that had been done by him, doctors' opinions of the man – until I got an idea of what I thought the person was like. And then I tried to bring it into a three-dimensional character.

127

My profession really is a lot of work. Katharine Hepburn once told Spencer Tracy, after she had seen a film of his called *Bad Day at Black Rock*, where he did a karate fight and really destroyed Ernie Borgnine: 'That karate fight was quite exceptional. Where did you learn that?' And he said: 'I thought about it.' And I thought that was a really exceptional concept of what actors do – he thought about it. He didn't need the actual experience as much as he needed the concept of it.

RUSSELL: Wasn't the Strangler murdered recently?

CURTIS: About three weeks ago. In a cell. Incredible man. There, he's gone now, you see, gone.

RUSSELL: Someone else who has been gone for a time and is being resurrected, by Mr Norman Mailer, is Miss Marilyn Monroe, whom you knew well. What do you think Mailer is doing for her at the moment?

CURTIS: He's done absolutely nothing for her. Why don't they let that poor girl lie dead? Why resurrect it? Why drag it up?

RUSSELL: Have you written about her at all?

CURTIS: No, I haven't. I've got nothing to write about her. She was a period of time; she was a contemporary of mine, someone that lived at the same period of time. We worked together, knew each other.

RUSSELL: Was it a pleasant experience?

CURTIS: Some of it was pleasant and some of it was not. But that's nobody's business but my own. There's another guy that wrote a book about Marilyn. He met her once. Norman Mailer never met her. Don't you love these people writing books about people they never met?

RUSSELL: Do people write books about you at all?

CURTIS: I don't know. I've never read one.

RUSSELL: I don't know whether this is true, but you've been quoted as saying about yourself that if you hadn't been an actor, you could have easily been a criminal.

CURTIS: Out of my background I could have been. I learned at a very early age that one doesn't really respect the law; that it is still a question of self-preservation and how do you survive? In New York City it was a tough haul when I was a kid. It's tougher now. But it's tough everywhere, you know. But those are the seediest parts of life; life is really much more pleasant.

RUSSELL: Why have you elected to come and live amongst us in London?

CURTIS: I like England. I like London. I find the people most pleasant, very interesting, very intelligent, individual – every person one meets.

RUSSELL: Are we less rude than Americans?

CURTIS: It's not a matter of being rude – I just like it here. I've just written two books and am now putting them together to be published. I paint a lot . . . I raise children, flowers, plants and chickens.

RUSSELL: Do you get rid of tensions and phobias and fears by painting?

CURTIS: No, I don't. It's a great pleasure, that after a number of years you're able to develop a style for yourself, and your hand does what your mind wants it to do. It doesn't happen by accident. Picasso said once to some painters that you must be very careful of the accidents, because by accident you may paint something that looks very nice. And you may think for a moment that you're pretty good. Forget it.

RUSSELL: If you had an exhibition, how would you feel the next morning reading *The Times*, the *Financial Times* . . .

CURTIS: And they say it stinks? I'd say: 'Well, read some of my movie reviews. Join the club.' I don't use critics as a means of telling me whether I think it's good or it's not good. The butcher can tell me that. I don't need some bum sitting behind a typewriter to give me that information.

RUSSELL: Well, I have to tell you that I have rarely been treated to such a dazzling display of self-confidence as that which has flown out of you tonight.

CURTIS: And vice versa. Thank you.

(*audience laughter; applause*)

JIMMY YOUNG

RUSSELL: Here he is to talk to me, and to sing, and he makes it all sound so easy, and his name is Mr Jimmy Young.
(*music; applause*)

> (*Jimmy Young sings 'It's So Easy'*)

(*applause*)

JIMMY YOUNG: (*laughing*) Quite a surprise, wasn't it?

RUSSELL: You know, listening to you like that makes me think I'm driving to work in the morning with my car radio on.

JIMMY YOUNG: It'll never replace music though, will it?

RUSSELL: No, but I think it's going a good way towards it. What do people think of you as?

JIMMY YOUNG: I don't know really. I suppose just a sort of ordinary guy who happens to be there in the home, I should think.

RUSSELL: Right. Now — well — the question I often ask people who are sitting in that chair, is, you know in the front of a passport you have to write your name, and your age and your occupation?

JIMMY YOUNG: Yes. Company Director.

RUSSELL: What? Is that what you put as your profession?

JIMMY YOUNG: Well, it's easy, isn't it? Yes.

RUSSELL: Yes — but supposing there were another line which said . . .

JIMMY YOUNG: Broadcaster . . .

RUSSELL: Yes — but supposing there were another line which said, er — 'Describe your character', so that a customs man could recognise you — which is a difficult question. How would you get out of that?

JIMMY YOUNG: Well, I'm an ordinary sort of a guy really. I'm just an ordinary guy doing an out-of-the-ordinary job.

RUSSELL: But that's blatantly untrue. You can't be an ordinary guy and reach all the people you reach.

JIMMY YOUNG: Yes, of course I can, and that is perhaps why I reach them in fact.

RUSSELL: But then why isn't the person next door doing it, or the man who lives in the flat upstairs?

JIMMY YOUNG: I don't know. There is obviously something which communicates itself. But if you were to ask me to describe it, I couldn't, and indeed if I could describe it, I wouldn't have it.

RUSSELL: Well, I can go some way to describing it for you, as it's clear you're embarrassed at describing it yourself.

JIMMY YOUNG: No, no. It's not that I'm embarrassed – no, I'm not embarrassed. I just literally can't do it.

RUSSELL: All right, then one of the things that distinguishes you from the man upstairs, or the guy who lives next door is that you're developing rapidly, and have developed rapidly a kind of 'banter'. Your J.Y. 'banter'. You've gone in for initials in a big way.

JIMMY YOUNG: Although they've disappeared, you know, recently. Well, over the last year or so. Not deliberately, they just have.

RUSSELL: But you see, you do know very cleverly how to use language, don't you?

JIMMY YOUNG: I don't, actually, you know. I just sit there.

RUSSELL: Oh, come on.

JIMMY YOUNG: No, honestly, I really promise you, I mean I just sit there and I talk, and out it comes. So do you for that matter.

RUSSELL: Yes, but I don't develop these strange kinds of mannerism and affectations of language, which work, which catch on.

JIMMY YOUNG: Well, yeah. It's not as simple as that, you see. The thing is, when I took the show round the Common Market, for instance, that was an entirely different scene, and yet it worked because it was a communication scene.

RUSSELL: Are you any kind of chameleon? Do you find it easy to change your colour wherever you are?

JIMMY YOUNG: No – I would say I'm always pretty well exactly as I am. I mean, I'm on now as I would be if you and I were having a gin and tonic, and talking round the corner

RUSSELL: Right. Now, no one can deny your popularity, and strange things are happening in radio, like a whole new commercial radio set-up is coming into focus. Have you been wooed at all by that?

JIMMY YOUNG: Oh, of course I have, and indeed I would have been very upset if I hadn't been (*laughing*). Yeah, I was offered – well, at any rate, three jobs which would have involved administration as well as broadcasting.

RUSSELL: But your loyalty is fixed.

JIMMY YOUNG: Well I've signed a three-year contract with the BBC, of which I've done a year, and I'm very happy with them – they're nice people to work for.

RUSSELL: They're all right. Where did you go to school?

JIMMY YOUNG: I went to school at East Dean Grammar School, which is in Gloucestershire, in the Forest of Dean, which is where I was born, and where my mother lived until she died last June.

RUSSELL: Yes. Was it a happy time, or an ordinary time?

JIMMY YOUNG: What, school?

RUSSELL: Yes.

JIMMY YOUNG: Not altogether, and indeed I ran away from home when I was fifteen.

RUSSELL: For what reason?

JIMMY YOUNG: Well basically because my home broke up. It was as simple as that.

RUSSELL: You haven't had very good luck in homes that you've lived in, and homes that you've tried to create, have you?

JIMMY YOUNG: No, I've not. It seems to be my ability to make other people happy, or cheer other people up, but no — you're quite right, I've not been fortunate in my emotional life.

RUSSELL: Where does the responsibility for that lie?

JIMMY YOUNG: I don't know. I would've thought ultimately with me. You know I can't be right and everybody else wrong. It must in the end come down to me. I am very obsessed with my job. There was an interesting quote actually by Tommy Steele in a Sunday paper a couple of weeks ago, where he said that he realised that he was obsessed with his job to the extent of it being an illness. And I think a lot of us are, in fact, in this business.

RUSSELL: Are you difficult to work with?

JIMMY YOUNG: *I* think I'm easy to work with, but that probably means I'm difficult (*laughs*).

RUSSELL: But if things don't go like that for you (*snaps fingers*), or if the microphone fails, or whatever . . . do you get short-tempered?

JIMMY YOUNG: Oh no, no. Oh no, not that sort of thing, no. I mean I'm a perfectionist on the job, but a mike going down or — or something. No, that doesn't bother me at all.

RUSSELL: How about fans? Do you have trouble or difficulty with fans?

JIMMY YOUNG: Well they vary. There are ladies who send me food parcels every week, because they think I need looking after. That's one end of the scale. On the other end there's a very tall hotel next to Broadcasting House, and I was up on the seventeenth floor there one day having a drink. I was about to leave, and there was a young lady, about twenty-two, I suppose, who was going to leave at the same time so I held the lift for her, being the old-world gentleman that I am, and she got in. She had this raincoat on, and I pressed the lift and down we started to go, and she said, quite conversationally, 'I'll bet you've never been in a lift before with a girl with no clothes on,' and I said, 'No, I can't say that I have', and – er – she undid the raincoat, and I was!

(*audience laughter*)

She then – she then leapt across the lift, you see, and there's not a lot of room for manoeuvring in a lift. I had my back against the buttons, and we got to the ground floor and she leaned over my shoulder and pressed the button, and we went back up again! Em – so I had another seventeen floors of it, until we got to the top floor, and I leapt out and I've not seen her from that day to this. But it's quite a hairy experience actually.

(*audience laughter*)

RUSSELL: Well, before the conversation goes either up or down again, may I say to you, Jimmy Young, thank you very much indeed.

JIMMY YOUNG: Thank you.

(*applause*)

MOLLY PARKIN

RUSSELL: American authoress Jacqueline Susann has made a fortune out of the misfortunes of her heroines. Molly Parkin, the fashion writer in one of the Sunday papers until recently, has set out to do the same thing. Now the only difference is that the misdemeanours of Molly Parkin's heroines are said to be auto-biographical. Ladies and gentlemen, here to defend herself is Molly Parkin.

(*music; applause*)

Now, have you actually got rid of your fashion work altogether? Have you put it to one side?

MOLLY: Yes.

RUSSELL: Why? Were you bored with it?

MOLLY: Yes, and I think fashion is a young person's game, anyway, and when I hit forty, I thought, 'It's time to look for another career.' Because if you are forty and still addicted to what people are putting on their bodies, I think that there's something wrong somewhere. Although it was a very cosy job, in a position of power, I thought it was time to call a halt.

RUSSELL: Was that a big decision, or did it grow gradually?

MOLLY: It grew gradually. It grew from the very first minute that I went into fashion – because I went into fashion as a relatively old woman anyway. I mean, I went into it when I was about thirty-two, and that's too old for a start-off.

RUSSELL: One of the things which you said, which struck me as being intensely interesting, is that when you do a job like the one you have been doing, fashion writer, you start to look at everybody and put them in immediate boxes and categories.

MOLLY: Yes.

RUSSELL: And that strikes me as an interesting thing – I had never thought of an occupational hazard.

MOLLY: Yes, you can look at them from top to toe, and you know exactly what they've spent on what they're wearing. I mean you can look at somebody and say – you know – '£7.10 Marks and Spencers', or '£17.10 Biba', or – you know – 'Harrods!' You can tell also with the face, how much they've spent on their face.

RUSSELL (*pointing at his own clothes*): All right, go ahead then Molly. (*audience laughter*)

MOLLY: Ladies, not gentlemen!

RUSSELL: Oh well, come on, I mean, you don't categorise . . .

MOLLY: Oh, I wouldn't like to go into that (*laughs*). I might suggest Gucci shoes, or at least copies of Gucci, anyway.

RUSSELL: Otherwise, I'm all right? Otherwise I'm o.k., you think, then?

MOLLY: Yes, very good.

RUSSELL: Right, right . . . Now, so you left fashion, and made a deliberate choice, and you've now finished your first book.

MOLLY: Yes.

RUSSELL: The book's called *Love All*.

MOLLY: Yes. I had thought originally to call it *Old Age Pensioners Are Free*, but the publishers didn't like that (*laughs*). And so, they said, 'Go away and think of something else,' and so I thought of that one. And they were very pleased with that, because they said anything with 'love' in it sells something like 80,000 more copies than it would if it didn't have 'love' in the title.

RUSSELL: Really?

MOLLY: Yes. That was something I didn't know.

RUSSELL: What kind of research can people possibly do into that kind of thing? Do you believe statements of that kind of magnitude?

MOLLY: I think I do, because anything with 'love' in the title does pull me as well. It's a book written for women, you see. Men, all the men that have read it, well, most of the men that read it get a little bit uneasy about it, because they think it's very offensive . . . and it is a little bit offensive for men.

RUSSELL: Well, I wouldn't say a *little* bit.

MOLLY: Oh well, very much offensive . . . to men.

RUSSELL: I walked up and down my bedroom at night with it on the end of a long thing, if you see what I mean. (*audience laughter*)

MOLLY: Well, it is worrying, of course, for men.

RUSSELL: What is the story of it, briefly?

MOLLY: Oh, I don't think it's got a story, has it?

RUSSELL: It's an odyssey, isn't it?

MOLLY: Is it?

RUSSELL: Well, it's a journey through a certain part of a person's life.

135

MOLLY: Yes, it's a journey through a week – it only takes place in a week.

RUSSELL: Right.

MOLLY: But it's lovely for women you see, because it's very joyous, and it actually goes into the fact that during sexual intercourse – however wonderful and rhapsodic it could be—you generally read that you should be seeing fleecy pink clouds and things, like cotton wool, and that there should be a heavenly chorus going on up there – but if she's got a perfectly good sexual encounter with somebody, and er. . . she's thinking about her children's school reports,

(*outburst of laughter*)

and she's thinking about, you know, cauliflower cheese and things like that, and in that way it's very nice, because it shows that the chap knows what he's doing, because he's relaxed her.

(*more laughter; applause*)

And I think women like that, you know. It's when they're not relaxed, or when they're with the men who are particularly unhappy lovers, as it were, and insensitive, that they get in a terrible state, so that they can't think of anything except 'When is it going to finish?'

I think *that's* true to say. And that's why all the women who've read it are very keen on the book. I mean it's a comic, erotic book, but above all it's comic: it's meant to make you laugh. And the gentlemen who don't laugh when they read it, you know – perhaps it's striking home, a little bit (*laughs*). I am glad you laughed. Perhaps you didn't laugh?

(*audience laughter*)

RUSSELL: I got confused in the cauliflower cheese bit, you see. I was looking for a flight of pink flamingoes, but they didn't turn up.

MOLLY: No, there *are* no flights in it.

RUSSELL: Has your husband told you what he is thinking of, when you're – er – together?

MOLLY: I don't like to ask him.

RUSSELL: Well, you could get him to write it down for you one night!

MOLLY: No, I'm too concerned with myself. I think that if I get myself sorted out, it doesn't so much matter what he is thinking of (*laughs*).

RUSSELL: Are you using the book, therefore, in any sense as therapy?

MOLLY: No. I held myself back with that book, to make it as decent as I possibly could.

(*audience laughter*)

Though I wanted to write a dirty book. It is true to say that I set out to write an extremely dirty book. And then I thought, 'better not put that', and I kept pulling back all the time. And now of course, people have said of it – 'It's poignant', and 'It's very moving.'

RUSSELL: That's quite true.

MOLLY: I'm very upset about that, because I set out to write the dirty book.

RUSSELL: Ah! Ah! You betrayed yourself earlier, by saying that comedy and erotic love are not altogether too wide apart. I mean, that we can find joy in sex, and we can celebrate sexual activity with a smile on our face – it doesn't have to be lewd.

MOLLY: Yes, but I wanted it to be a very coarse smile you see! I wanted it to be very coarsely funny. And when people talk in that way of it being poignant, then I fall back to being with all the women novelists of our time, good ladies though they are. But I don't wish to be that poignant, rather 'crucified-in-the-womb' sort of writer. I don't wish to be that.

RUSSELL: How much of this is subconsciously kicking against the Welsh hills? Because that's where you sprang from, isn't it?

MOLLY: Yes, it is.

RUSSELL: Have you thought about that?

MOLLY: Born in the shadow of the chapel? . . . It's true.

RUSSELL: I bet it sells like hot cakes in that valley!

MOLLY: Oh, I don't think so.

RUSSELL: Oh come on . . . they'll all be buying it and wrapping it under plain cover and passing it round, I bet.

MOLLY: Oh, I hope so – well, not passing it round: buying their own. My mother's actually just been up – she comes from there – and I said to her: 'Don't read it. You'll get yourself very upset if you do that. Not even the first line.' (Because the first line is very rude.) And she said, 'I'll just take it up, I've got my glasses, and have a look at it in bed.' And then the next day, it was half read, and I said, 'How are you getting on with it? I said not to read it.' She said, 'Oh I 'ope Auntie Emmie doesn't have a look at it. She's very old-fashioned.' She's in her eighties, and my mother's in her seventies! (*audience laughter*)

RUSSELL: How consciously have you smashed it target-wise at the Jacqueline Susann market?

MOLLY: Oh I don't know. I think it's a bit dirtier than her books and in that way, you know, could come up against a lot of trouble. It really could come to be like an underground – you know, word-of-mouth-novel.

RUSSELL: You're doing a good hard sell on it, Molly, aren't you?

137

You really are.

MOLLY: I hope so.

RUSSELL: You had a marvellous granny, didn't you? A marvellous Welsh granny.

MOLLY: How do you know that?

RUSSELL: Well, it's my job to know certain things about you, isn't it? One of the nicest things about your granny, which you may not know, and which I may tell the audience, is that whenever she was washing her knickers . . .

MOLLY: Yes?

RUSSELL: She used to take the elastic out, to save it, so she didn't get it warped.

MOLLY: Yes.

RUSSELL: Do you, do you suffer from that kind of . . .

MOLLY: No.

RUSSELL: I'm not saying do you *do* that, I'm saying do you have economic thrust at the back of your mind?

MOLLY: No. But you see, I come from a mining valley, and all my relatives are either postmen, teachers or miners. And my grandmother was very ambitious, and she saw the only way to get out of her environment was to own it. And she used to take the elastic out of her knickers, because she was saving money. You know the knickers would rot, but she still had the elastic for you know, going on, and so she managed to buy house after house, street after street, in this little mining village. So she came to be a landowner, and when people say to me, 'Your background, you know, is obviously working-class, very humble,' I say 'I come from landowners!'

RUSSELL: I love the thought of your granny standing in a street saying, 'See all that? I bought that from knicker elastic!' I think it's marvellous. Are you enjoying your life, now, today? I don't mean necessarily at this moment, but this *time* of your life?

MOLLY: Yes, it's wonderful. I wrote in the newspaper that I work for that life begins at forty, because that's what the song says, and it really did happen for me. And I'd like a lot of women to know that, because there's such a youth cult at the minute — and I've got teenage daughters — but if you can let yourself go, and push on and that, it can get better as you get older, because by then you don't care what people are thinking anyway.

RUSSELL: Which fact you have ably demonstrated tonight, Molly Parkin.

(*applause*)

138

OLIVER REED

RUSSELL: I'd like you to meet someone who's said to believe in leprechauns, and who cherishes Winnie the Pooh. He used to be a nightclub bouncer, and it's no secret that there are thousands of girls who would bounce in his direction if only he would give them the word. Ladies and gentlemen, the man once described as the Errol Flynn of Wimbledon Common, Mr Oliver Reed.

(*music; applause*)

Now, do girls *still* bounce at you, or towards you?

REED: No, because I breed horses and they're frightened of the horses, which is a shame.

RUSSELL: But does that mean you don't get troubled by them at all?

REED: No. I'm a liar, too.

(*audience laughter*)

RUSSELL: Thank God. In any kind of woman who crosses your eye vision, do brains attract you more than breasts?

REED: No.

(*audience laughter*)

No. I did a programme on television a few months ago with a Woman's Liberationist, and I decided then that I didn't . . . She kept on spitting. (*Russell laughs.*) And I didn't find that very attractive, and then there were lots of people shouting . . .

RUSSELL: Wait a minute, spitting in what way?

REED: Spitting at *me*. Then she kept on calling me a male chauvinist pig, and she said I couldn't stand up unless there was a woman holding me. And so from that time on I decided that I would go without the brains and go back to the breasts.

(*audience laughter*)

I don't really like being bludgeoned over the head with some woman's *Reader's Digest* intellect. I really don't. I think that women are superb. I adore them. But I don't want to know how clever they are—I think it's incidental. I think it should be for any intelligent woman: either her anatomy or her brain should be incidental to a relationship.

139

RUSSELL: But if her anatomy is attractive to you and is in any way usable by you – *after* that using, isn't it a further attractive prospect to be able to talk pleasurably with her?

REED: Yes, it is. 'I say, do you want breakfast?' Or, 'Would you like a cup of tea?'

(*audience laughter*)

And as long as they can say 'Yes' or 'No', that's o.k.

RUSSELL (*laughing*): That's all they need to say?

REED: Yes, sure.

RUSSELL: Now, you seem to float across life quite comfortably. You don't seem to have any deep problems that pull you back, or pull you down. You seem to enjoy life. You seem to be a *bon viveur*. Would that be a reasonably accurate description of you?

REED: I think you'd have to ask the police about that. Yes, I enjoy life very much. It's just that sometimes my humour doesn't seem to appeal to the Spanish, the Bulgarians or the Romanians. I think that an Englishman has a different sense of humour. I was arrested in Spain because I was Indian wrestling with a Finn who was 7 foot 2. I thought he seemed like a good fellow to wrestle with. Unfortunately, the table broke and we fell into the ice-cream trolley . . . The ice-cream went over an American lady's dress, so the husband picked up a bun and threw it at me. So I picked up the glacé cherry and threw it at him.

(*audience laughter*)

Then all of a sudden fifteen boys came in dressed as policemen, with machine guns, and they dragged me off. And they woke up a judge at half past three in the morning, because the hotel insisted that something should be done about it. I couldn't speak Spanish, so I said, 'Tres Musketeer . . . el Musketeer,' and they thought I was going to attack them.

So five boys jumped on my arm again, and I was taken into this great empty courtroom with the judge sitting there, who was very cross at being woken up so early in the morning. In the end, he gave it up and just shook his head and smiled. And he said, 'Just tell him to leave your hotel.' And so I was thrown out on to the streets with my bags.

RUSSELL: All life seems to be a kind of adventure to you, doesn't it?

REED: I think it should be. I think that everybody would like that. It's just that very few people have the opportunity.

RUSSELL: But thank God there are people like you through whom we can actually live vicariously. Do you know what I mean?

REED: Yeah. What's that mean? (*laughs*)

RUSSELL: Well, it means that we can enjoy the bravado of your life or aura of your life, while you're doing it for us at second hand.

REED: Yeah.

RUSSELL: You get into a lot of fights in the film of *The Three Musketeers*.

REED: Yup.

RUSSELL: Were they real fights?

REED: Yup.

RUSSELL: Who do you fight with?

REED: I fight with some of the cardinal's guards and I fight with Christopher Lee. In actual fact I got run through for real – fighting Christopher's double. Christopher was asked to throw himself on the floor, and he hurt his leg, and so I fought his double. And the double hadn't rehearsed the fight properly. He was supposed to stab me underneath the left arm, and so I came round to take the blow, and as I came round he stabbed me under the right arm . . .

RUSSELL: Oh my God!

REED: . . . and my hand was in the way and it went through my hand and out the other side.

RUSSELL: What happened then?

REED: I went to hospital, got blood poisoning . . .

(*audience laughter*)

. . . and the hospital food was terrible, as it usually is, and so I got my fat friend Reg Prince to smuggle me in pizzas through the hospital window.

(*audience laughter*)

And my girl-friend used to climb in through the window as well, so we used to have parties at night.

RUSSELL: There were many film stars on the set of *The Three Musketeers*, but I presume they were never all there together, were they?

REED: There were a great many of them there at the inauguration, which is the final scene of the first half of the film.

RUSSELL: How easily do you find it is to work with large numbers of stars? Are you a person who works and fits in easily with other people?

REED: I don't think that's for me to say. On the set I don't have a lot of actors as friends, because I believe that our interests are the same, and therefore I'd much rather talk to people whose interests are different to mine. I have more to learn – or more to say. I can't talk to actors about acting because they know about it and it's boring, but

I don't mind talking to a milkman about acting. I gave my hat to my milkman – my musketeer's hat. He collects hats, and has a hundred and fifty of them.

RUSSELL: Did you get on terribly well with Raquel? There was a story filtered back that Raquel was deeply interested – Raquel Welch, that is . . .

REED: Yeah. I hired a pub, which seemed like a good idea, as a thank you to the crew at the end of the film. And it so happened that Raquel was just starting the film and she had failed to receive an invitation. So I had to hurriedly send one out and she appeared with her hairdresser. I danced with the hairdresser and – it's like one of those terrible Dudley Moore and Peter Cook jokes – I said, "Course, she sulked all night,' and the Press immediately said that – that she was sulking because I didn't dance with her. No, I'm sure she's got many more people she'd like to dance with than me. I want to put that straight, Raquel. She's very fond of me, really.

RUSSELL: Is she?

(*audience laughter*)

And you of her?

REED: Oh, very deeply.

RUSSELL: Now, you're talking about not wanting to spend much time talking to actors. You also have, in the distant past, proclaimed that you have a disregard for things like drama schools, – that you didn't yourself need any kind of dramatic training in your early days.

REED: I think that drama school is ideal for people that need drama school. I think that in the 'fifties when I started to act, everybody had a particular style, which was fine for the 'fifties. And then came Marlon Brando and Paul Newman, and actors like Finney started to develop a style of their own, which was to do nothing. So that's what I do – I do nothing, and I'm sure that had I gone to drama school people would have tried to make me do something. You take your photographs round to all the agents, but they're not terribly concerned whether or not you've been to drama school – to RADA, or to Central School – they are concerned about the fact that you might have done something that they can see. And if you've done nothing, they can't see it – it's the same old story.

RUSSELL: How did *you* break into it then?

REED: I was an extra – a film extra, and I went round and I lied to everybody. I said that I was in a repertory company in South Africa and in Australia – in Wagamoomoo . . .

(*audience laughter*)

. . . hoping that they wouldn't be able to check up—and they didn't. And then I started at Hammer, which was my repertory company. They gave me my first parts.

RUSSELL: In horror?

REED: In horror, yeah.

RUSSELL: Can you spell?

REED: No. That's why I'm an actor.

(*audience laughter*)

RUSSELL: But is that not an affectation? I mean, supposing you have to write a private note to a girlfriend . . .?

REED: Yeah.

RUSSELL: Does somebody write it for you, or do you declare your intention phonetically?

REED: No, I telephone her.

(*audience laughter*)

I'm terrible. And my son—it suddenly dawned on me—my son has gone to boarding school, and the embarrassment is that I have to send him post-cards, and I don't know how to spell! And obviously, the masters, when they're dealing out the mail must read them, and there's your actual Oliver Reed writing to his son and he can't spell. So I've given up writing postcards now.

RUSSELL: Does it not embarrass your son, that?

REED: Well, you should see *his* spelling.

(*audience laughter*)

My goodness, it's costing me a fortune. He's the most expensive illiterate I know, God bless him.

RUSSELL: Did you have a good life in the army?

REED: I enjoyed the army. I wasn't a very successful soldier. They thought I was taking the mickey out of them, because they said I sounded like an officer but I spelt like a yob, you see, which I was very proud of. And so they sent me to see a psychiatrist, who said that my parents were divorced and that's why I couldn't spell, which was why I wasn't an officer. So I ended up cleaning the ablutions!

RUSSELL: What, for the entire time?

REED: No, it was when I was on fatigues. And then they posted me as far away from anywhere as they could get, which was the Far East, and I served over there.

RUSSELL: I can't say 'Did you have a good war?', because you weren't in the war, but you know what I mean,—did you have a good National Service?

REED: I thought then that National Service was a bit of a waste of time. They could have increased the amount of money they paid the soldiers and enticed a more technically skilled and able man into the army. – They now have a Regular Army, and they get paid a great deal of money. I think that it was an experience, but it was two years I could have done without.

RUSSELL: Is there anything deep down that you care passionately about?

REED: I care passionately about Great Britain when I'm abroad. Yes, I get very patriotic. I care about my rugby club, and I care . . .

RUSSELL: Your local rugby club?

REED: Rosslyn Park. Because they're a good load of lads. And I care about England.

RUSSELL: It's a very grand big claim, that.

REED: You asked me.

RUSSELL: Yes, but I was wondering if you cared about things which are smaller. Like – if you care about animals, apart from your horses. Do you have a private domestic pet?

REED: We have fifteen horses at home and six dogs and six cats and three doves and a tame gardener.

(*audience laughter*)

RUSSELL: And you stroke them all at one time or another, do you? (*Oliver Reed laughs.*)

I'd like to ask you finally, or almost finally, about the twenty years which you have predicted for your future life. You say you want six years of total insecurity, followed by six years of sexual abandon, followed by six years of senility followed then, which I don't understand, by two years of understanding.

REED: Yes, the two years of understanding: I don't think that if you understand everything you could survive more than two years, could you? I mean, directly Jesus Christ did, they crucified Him.

RUSSELL: Yes, but Oliver, are you pushing any analogy there? (*audience laughter*)

REED: I'm just trying to say I'm smart. I just want to see your reaction. I thought it was one of these intelligent shows we were on.

No, I don't know. I must have been pissed when I said that . . . I can't really work it out.

(*audience laughter*)

I think that for the next twenty years, it depends how life treats me, doesn't it? I mean, how can one plan that? I think I would like to make children's films. I would like to make imagination films,

144

because I have such good ideas when I'm in the pub. Then when I wake up in the morning I find that they're all imagination. But in actual fact one *can* put them into a reality, build them into a reality – which means film them . . .

RUSSELL: Mmm.

REED: So I'm going to play a big fat clown that wanders through the stinging nettles talking to imaginary animals (*pauses*). Because I believe in er, as you said, goblins. Silver ones, anyway, I don't believe in gold ones any more, because they had a war with the – er, with the cobblers.

RUSSELL: When?

REED: Oh, last year. It was terrible. On Trafalgar Day.

(*audience laughter*)

RUSSELL: Did you witness any of this?

REED: Yes I did. That's why I don't believe in them any more. The gold ones lost, – they ran.

RUSSELL: Are the silver ones bigger than the gold ones?

REED: Much much bigger.

RUSSELL: What kind of hats do the silver ones wear?

REED: Silver.

(*audience laughter*)

And they run very fast. They leave a great trail of silver behind them. In actual fact I saw that one night. It was snowing and I'm sure it was a dog running very fast, but the way the moon was – no, so I believed in them then. And then a journalist came down and talked to me about it and persuaded me that I was going out of my mind, so I gave up goblins (*pauses*). That's why I breed horses.

RUSSELL (*laughing*): Oliver Reed, thank you very much indeed.

REED: Thank you.

(*applause*)

145

ELTON JOHN

RUSSELL: Now my next guest has just arrived back from an exhausting world concert tour. He once called himself 'the electric Liberace', but Liberace never wore windscreen wipers on his sun-glasses, did he? Ladies and gentlemen, Mr Elton John.

(*applause; cheers; music*)

Is it giving anything away to say that I would like everybody to wish you a happy birthday? It's his birthday, ladies and gentlemen.

ELTON: Twenty-four again.

RUSSELL: Again! Are you a steady twenty-four?

ELTON: A steady twenty-four. It's a good age to be.

RUSSELL: Would you like to explain to a panting nation why you've called yourself Hercules?

ELTON: Well, when I changed my name from Reginald Kenneth Dwight to Elton John, by deed poll, I just wanted a middle name, so the only thing I could think of was Steptoe's horse, which was called Hercules. So I thought, nobody ever uses their middle names really unless you're sort of royalty or titled, so . . .

RUSSELL: Or the President of the United States.

ELTON: Quite right, so I just had it. My mother went crazy. She hated it.

RUSSELL: She did?

ELTON: 'Oh, that's Steptoe's horse!' she said. No one ever uses it, but it's the title of one of our songs as well.

RUSSELL: But it's got nothing to do with muscle and brawn?

ELTON: Certainly not. I'm one of the weakest people out, I tell you, folks.

RUSSELL: Are you? At home, do you have any of those muscle machines?

ELTON: No, not at all. No. I don't do any exercises at all apart from training with Watford, and – (had to get that one in, sorry) and just on stage. That's all the training I get, and the odd tennis match. But that's about it.

RUSSELL: But on stage, presumably, or in the middle of a concert, you lose a lot of weight?

ELTON: Yes, but then you see you sweat so much and you lose that amount of weight, and then you come off stage and have one Coca-cola and you put it all back on again, so, it doesn't really matter really. It just keeps you in trim. You don't *lose* weight. It's very hard to lose weight on tour.

RUSSELL: I suppose we're lucky in a sense to see you here at all because you've had one or two roughish experiences at the hands of — almost at the hands of the law, haven't you?

ELTON: I was arrested in New Zealand, yes, and for assault. I grabbed somebody by the shirt, which in New Zealand is one of the chief crimes of the nation, so I was arrested and acquitted, thank God. So. Oh, we had a little trouble in New Zealand. You have to realise that it's a Victorian sort of country and they don't really like English people very much. It's very anti-Pom.

RUSSELL: That's not what we've been led to believe, is it? — that they don't like English people or they don't like er . . . people of your sort?

ELTON: Oh, thank you very much. No, I think basically there is a great anti-Pom feeling especially when it comes to sport and things like that. I suppose because I am who I am, and I'm young and I earn a lot of money, *et cetera*, *et cetera*. Er — they're probably very anti what I stand for. We met a lot of nice people out there, but the general feeling was of — hostility — from the older sort of people.

RUSSELL: Even though — I presume the concerts were packed out?

ELTON: Well we played to — yeah we did a concert in New Zealand to 35,000 people which is one per cent of the population. The kids were marvellous. I'm going to go back to New Zealand, because you can't blame a country — you can't sort of have grudges against people just because two or three people were nasty to you. And most of the people we met there were really nice.

RUSSELL: Apart from England, which I presume you consider to be home, which is the country in the world where you feel most at home?

ELTON: I'd have to say America, because I spend so much time there . . . spend probably up to five or six months of the year there, so I consider Los Angeles is my second home, but I always consider England as home. It's always sort of a relief to land at London Airport.

RUSSELL: Now is Los Angeles as — to quote your own favourite word — *horrendous* as the rest of us are led to believe it is? A large, smog-ridden, conurbation where nothing happens?

ELTON: When you first go there, you love it. There's so much to do.

147

There's Disneyland and there's all the sights to see, and it's Holly-wood *et cetera, et cetera.* It's very sort of – well, 'really groovy and cosmic' you know, and there's a lot of people out there who are really sort of oh, very dreary, and they're so '*into*' everything: into hamburgers and . . .

(*audience laughter*)

. . . no matter what it is, 'Are you *into* that? Fabulous! I really love it.' You have to steer clear of that lot.

There're a lot of nice people out there. But there is a danger of falling into a clique in Los Angeles which is very groovy and it's really like a holocaust. It's sort of like Sodom and Gomorrah. I think one day it's going to go straight into the sea.

RUSSELL: But it'll have been worth while, probably.

ELTON: I don't know. But I enjoy it over there because I know lots of normal people, which is always helpful.

RUSSELL: I'm wondering whether the reason why from time to time you get into trouble – and you get into trouble marginally less than other people in your position – I'm thinking now of the Who and the Stones and people. Is it because you find it difficult to hold your-self decently back when you're provoked by so many people? I mean, you must be provoked by a hell of a lot of people.

ELTON: We are provoked a lot. I'm very placid, I'm very non-violent, usually. But if someone says 'We're going to beat you up and the rest of your group and everyone concerned with your party,' what do you do? I mean, you don't just say, 'Thank you very much, and goodnight, and I hope you have a nice night's sleep,' or something like that. You sort of turn round and say 'Why?'

We never had that happen to us except in Australia and New Zealand – ever. Even in America, which is supposed to be one of the most violent countries in the world. The only trouble we've ever had is in Australia and New Zealand.

RUSSELL: Do newspapers and journalists in particular irritate you or irk you? Or on the whole do you have a rapport with them?

ELTON: I think you have to grin and bear it. I mean I think I have a good relationship with the Press. There was a time when I didn't have a particularly good one, but I think I was a bit of a spoilt child then. I had so many good reviews, and then when you start to get the bad reviews you think, 'Oh, don't like them very much.' But you have to. You know that for six months you're going to be talked about well, and then the next six months they're going to have a go at you. It's paper policy – especially musical papers. They have to sell on controversy so they're just going to love you for six months and then hate you the next. I understand that now, so I have a pretty good relationship.

RUSSELL: Now, you have an immense reputation, public and private, for being a generous person. Not only are you generous to other people, or seemingly so, though I haven't had a present from you yet . . .

ELTON: I gave you a kiss backstage for the champagne. What more do you want?

(*audience laughter*)

RUSSELL: I don't want the world to know about it! But apart from that, you seem to be extremely generous to *yourself*. You adorn your body fairly richly.

ELTON: If you had a body like mine so would you.

(*audience laughter*)

RUSSELL: How many rings are you wearing, for instance, at the moment?

ELTON: Three.

RUSSELL: Are those real diamonds?

ELTON: They're real – yeah, they're real diamonds, Russell.

RUSSELL: Are they really a 'girl's best friend'? is what I was going to ask you.

ELTON: Not really, no. It's just a bit of me coming out, yes.

RUSSELL: But are you generous to people because you feel that you want to share the money that you've got, and the happiness that you've got, or is it to *buy* some kind of thing?

ELTON: Oh no. I think my great philosophy of life is that I could be knocked over by a bus tomorrow, something could happen to change my life tomorrow that would mean that it was all over. I can't understand anyone hoarding money just for the sake of it, or for a rainy day, because by the time the rainy day gets there, there's no one to enjoy it with, because everyone's died off. So you might as well enjoy it while you can. So – if I am knocked over by a car tomorrow, Russell, I leave you this ring, I promise (*laughs*).

RUSSELL: Get that down, somebody, in writing, I want you to write it. Are you fond of big cars?

ELTON: It's a weakness with me, actually. I do like cars, yes.

RUSSELL: Do you drive yourself?

ELTON: Sort of – yeah, I do, and I've got someone who drives me as well, because I don't like driving in London very much.

RUSSELL: No. But it's a great joy is it, to you, to get into a fast car along a straight road?

149

ELTON: Oh yeah, I like driving geared cars. Like really fast geared cars.

RUSSELL: There was a time when your Mum was embarrassed about going out in the street with you when you were dressed somewhat like . . .

ELTON: She still is, I tell you. There was a point when Carnaby Street was selling all those military uniforms and everyone was walking around in army trench-coats. I went to a jumble sale and bought one for 50p, and it had all holes in it and it was down to the ground, and I thought it was fantastic. I went up to my mother at the local shops in Northwood Hills and said, 'Hullo, mum,' and she said, 'I'm not walking home with you in that.'

(*audience laughter*)

And she walked on one side of the street and I walked on the other.

RUSSELL: Is your mum in any sense critical of any of the music that you make or . . .

ELTON: Oh yes, oh yeah: 'Too loud. Too loud. Can't hear the voice'—specially when she comes to the concerts. She likes the slow ones—you know, the quieter things. She likes a bit of rock and roll as well, but I mean she always says things are too loud or 'No, I don't like that one. Never have liked that one.' That's great, because as I say she's a mum and she's honest, you know.

RUSSELL: Now, you've talked about Hollywood a bit and about Los Angeles. You are a friend of Mae West's, it has been reported.

ELTON: Not a friend, I've only met her twice. I've been to tea twice, so I would hardly class myself or dare to class myself as a friend. We were invited for an 'audience', as it's called, I think. It was fantastic. It really was an 'audience'.

RUSSELL: Please tell me about it.

ELTON: Well, the first time I went, there were six of us, six guys, and we were shown into her apartment in Hollywood, which is all white, has white everyting: white piano, white sofa—everything's white. And you sit there for about five minutes and a Chinese man comes through and says, 'Gentlemen, Miss West'. And she swishes in looking fantastic, and she looks at you and goes, 'Mmm, wall to wall man.'

(*audience laughter*)

I was trying to look for the face lift, but I mean she looks *fantastic*. And the hands, you know I looked at the hands and they're beautiful and smooth and she just looked exactly like she does on the screen. She's very, very interesting. She's very coherent and she's very much 'into' E.S.P.: 'I'm into E.S.P.' She tells you all about that — her experiences. And she likes health foods and carrot juice and things like that. Groucho Marx is another one: you just sit there and let them carry on. You can't say anything because they're so interesting, and the stories they've got to tell are just fantastic. I think she was so ahead of her time. She was banned on Broadway for a show which was called *Sex*, way back in the 1920s, I think, and she had to show it in New Jersey because they wouldn't let it on in New York.

RUSSELL: The show you mean?

ELTON: Yeah.

(*audience laughter*)

RUSSELL: Did she know who you were?

ELTON: Not really, no. Groucho Marx — I've met him about eight times and I've got a poster he signed for me at home, which is 'to John Elton' because he thinks I should spell my name the other way around. And it's 'To John Elton from Marx Groucho'.

(*audience laughter*)

He knows I play the piano: 'You're the guy that plays the piano' — and that's about it! No, they haven't really heard of me, no.

RUSSELL: You've had the distinction, have you not, of having had Katharine Hepburn in your swimming pool?

ELTON: Fishing out dead frogs, yes. While I stood quaking at the side going 'There's a frog in the pool, there's a frog in the pool.' (*laughs*)

(*audience laughter*)

RUSSELL: How did she come to be in your pool?

ELTON: Well, I live very close to Bryan Forbes who did our documentary and we're very friendly. He knows her — 'course, she's one of my idols as well — and we're having tea one day on the lawn, and up she cycles on the lawn, because at that point we didn't have any gates in front of the house. And oh, she just takes command, she's fantastic, she just takes over. And she goes for a swim and she does somersaults off the diving board. — I can't even dive in the pool — I sort of edge in very gracefully, or try to. And there was a dead frog in the pool. One thing in the world I'm frightened of is frogs, because they leap and you don't know where they're going. She hates frogs as well, but she just got this big twig, dived in the pool, fished it out and threw it. And . . .

RUSSELL: In whose direction?

ELTON: Well, not at me, thank God. But I said, 'Listen, h-h-how on earth could you do that?' And she just turned round, and you know, didn't say it for effect, she said, 'Character, dear boy. Character', and just started swimming again.

(*audience laughter*)

You know. It left me mesmerised (*laughs*).

RUSSELL: Have you written at all about all these people that you've met? I mean, there's obviously a book behind this, isn't there?

ELTON: Well, I've kept a diary for about five or six years.

RUSSELL: Oh, really. Is it a *daily* diary?

ELTON: A daily diary.

RUSSELL: I mean, you actually sit at night saying 'Dear Diary . . .'

ELTON: 'Dear Diary, I went up the shops today to get some Windolene, and they'd sold out.'

(*audience laughter*)

RUSSELL: Now the music we're going to hear tonight is called 'Candle in the Wind' and has a strong ambience of Marilyn Monroe, whom I presume you never met?

ELTON: No.

RUSSELL: But you're obviously – as they would say to you – in Sunset Boulevard – you're *into* Marilyn now, are you?

ELTON: Ah, well no, actually, it's really Bernie Taupin, you see. Everyone forgets that Bernie writes all the lyrics and I just write the melodies to the lyrics.

RUSSELL: Well, you're generous enough not to allow people to forget.

ELTON: Well, he's 'really into Marilyn Monroe, man', and you should probably talk to *him* about that. I'm a Marilyn Monroe fan too, but I think he's more 'into' Marilyn Monroe than I am, because he knows far more about her, and goes to auctions when they sell her things. I think that's terrible. You imagine, they had an auction in Los Angeles where you could buy her driving licence. It's very sad to think that nobody loved her enough to actually keep her driving licence.

RUSSELL: But that's one of the penalties of being a cult figure, Elton, isn't it?

ELTON: Well, she wasn't a cult figure while she was alive, I don't think. I don't think anyone is till they die. She was very popular, but when she died it was like the tragic Hollywood story, wasn't it? I mean, everybody loves a story like that.

RUSSELL: Well, we're looking forward now to hearing a song which is called 'Candle in the Wind'.

(*applause*)

ILIE NASTASE

RUSSELL: Here, ladies and gentlemen, is Ilie Nastase.
(*applause*)
How do you do?
NASTASE: Very well. (*Produces a bent racquet and a glass of orange juice.*) I brought the racquet I use to play with (*laughs*).
RUSSELL: Where did you get that into that shape?
NASTASE: Well, I keep it in my er . . . badroom.
RUSSELL: Bathroom.
NASTASE: Bathroom, bathroom.
RUSSELL: You keep it in your bathroom? Is this why it gets so. . . .
NASTASE: Yes.
RUSSELL: Because of the heat you have in your bathroom?
NASTASE: Yes.
RUSSELL: Not because of the heat in your bedroom?
NASTASE: No.
(*audience laughter*)
RUSSELL: I see. Why is it that the French, and the Italians, and the Romanians, and the Americans, i.e. other nations, like you less than we like you?
NASTASE: Well, maybe because I beat all the French, all the Italians. I never lose to the Italian and French.
(*applause*)
RUSSELL: But you see you win all the French tournaments, and that kind of thing, so they don't like you for that.
NASTASE: Maybe—I don't know.
RUSSELL: And also you steal out of France one of the jewels of their feminine crowns . . . What am I saying?
NASTASE: *I* don't say it (*laughing*). I think she steal me from Romania.
RUSSELL: She stole you, did she?
(*Nastase laughs*)
Where is she, at this moment?
NASTASE: Well, she is sick, but she has to go back to France.
RUSSELL: Where do you live? Where is your home?

NASTASE: Well, my home is in the hotels everywhere, because I play eleven months a year, so every week I'm in a different place.

RUSSELL: Do you travel everywhere by air?

NASTASE: Yes.

RUSSELL: But doesn't that make you feel sick?

NASTASE: I am sick always . . . when I'm flying. . . very much.

RUSSELL: What a terrible prospect though, because you have to go to so many places, and you travel with a sick-bag all the time.

NASTASE: Well, I'll go in a submarine, some day.

RUSSELL: But does that not make training difficult? I mean, when you fly long distances, your legs get tight, and your body is crumpled up in an aeroplane.

NASTASE: Yes, especially on a plane. You are a bit worried, you might win a tournament in one week, and finish on Sunday and next Monday you have to be in America or somewhere, so, it's very, very difficult to get in good condition to play.

RUSSELL: Mmm. Let's play a little game now, not tennis, but a little mind game — if suddenly, you were ordered to live only in one place, in the whole world — you could choose wherever you wanted to go in the world, but you couldn't ever move away from that — where would be your location?

NASTASE: I should say England.

RUSSELL: Now you're not just being diplomatic?

NASTASE: No, I'm not diplomatic.

RUSSELL: No, you're *not* diplomatic, that's evident!

(*applause*)

RUSSELL: Now you are, . . . if you'll forgive this, but when you're playing tennis, you are also aware of an audience, of a crowd of people who pay money to watch you. So that from time to time, you actually perform to people, don't you? Now is that a conscious thing?

NASTASE: I think it's just part of my game, it's natural, I never think about it, you know . . . it's my game.

RUSSELL: You swear a lot, don't you?

NASTASE: Er well, not in English.

(*audience laughter*)

When I'm here, I swear in Italian.

RUSSELL: Does the hostility of the crowd annoy you? Do you feel you have to fight that as well as your opponent?

NASTASE: Well, actually I like to play *against* the crowd. That makes me more concentrate. I like to fight against the crowd, you know. It's a different play.

RUSSELL: Can you remember the last time the crowd was really hostile?

NASTASE: Well, I think it is when I play last year in the United States, in the final of the American Open, against Arthur Ashe. Fifty thousand people were against me, and er . . . I am sorry to say, their linesman was a black man, and you know, he gave me a foot fault at a very difficult moment, very critical moment, and you know, I have to pass all these tests.

RUSSELL: But, it helps you to fight, doesn't it?

NASTASE: Yes.

RUSSELL: Does that mean the opposite is true? That when the audience is all shouting for you, you go limp completely?

NASTASE: Yes, you know, when I miss a ball, and all the girls they, you know, go like this (*sighs deeply*), it make you play like you sick.

RUSSELL: What does your wife think about the hero-worship that you get from all these young women?

NASTASE: Well, I don't know what she thinks but I think it's really too much. When you play important match, you know, it's hard to concentrate, and they like you to win—that's very fine—but they disturb you sometimes.

RUSSELL: You are also, on the court itself, a practical joker, aren't you? You like to make things lively. You like to wear odd things, and do odd things. Tell us a few of those.

NASTASE: I like to be relaxed sometimes, when everybody in the dressing-room is so nervous. I will come in my tricolour vest and moustache and all these things, and one day I was playing in America, and everybody wore a colour shirt, and I just come out with my shirt, which was my pyjama.

(*audience laughter*)

I was fined, the next day I was fined $50, but I enjoy it. Even though I was fined, I enjoy it so much.

RUSSELL: When you're fined, which you have been lots of times, you've been fined for other things as well.

NASTASE: Well, I was fined because I threw a ball to the linesman, but unfortunately I don't hit him.

RUSSELL: I don't think you mean 'threw the ball *to* the linesman', I think you mean 'threw the ball *at* the linesman'.

NASTASE: *At* the linesman, I am sorry my English is not . . .

RUSSELL: No, no, your English is very, very good . . . almost as good as your tennis.

155

NASTASE: Thank you, you're kind.

RUSSELL: Not at all. So you were fined for that?

NASTASE: So I miss him, and I have to pay in the States a fine of $100, because I miss him.

RUSSELL: They penalised you?

NASTASE: Yes.

RUSSELL: What kind of discipline do you inflict upon yourself? You bring orange juice. Does that mean you don't drink alcohol?

NASTASE: No, not really—I drink a few beers, you know. But I play so much I don't have time to. I don't have time to drink.

RUSSELL: When you're playing in big tournaments, say, like Wimbledon, how does that affect your love life? Do you, do you have . . . (laughs)

NASTASE: Well there are these sacrifice you know, like the sportsmen have to, even if you don't have to play that day, you have to practise hard.

RUSSELL: What are we talking about, your love-life?

NASTASE: No, no, no, tennis, tennis.

(audience laughter)

I spend all my day with socks on, you know.

RUSSELL: Right, right.

NASTASE: So if you don't practise, you have to play, so, . . . you have a racquet in your hand, and you arrive at eight-thirty home, or nine, your wife likes to have a beer, and you have a beer, and then you have to sleep, because the next day it will be something, so it is some kind of sacrifice.

RUSSELL: Business comes before pleasure.

NASTASE: Yes.

RUSSELL: What kind of insurance do you have for the future, because I mean, you're not going to be able to play tennis until you're sixty. Or maybe you're going to be the first person to be winning Wimbledon at sixty? Do you have plans for the future? When your tennis is finished? Or when your days as a tennis player are finished?

NASTASE: Well, depends how much I own, how much my winnings are. I don't know what I'm doing after.

RUSSELL: How much money you win, you mean?

NASTASE: Yes. So I don't know if I build on the tennis. I like to build on the tennis.

RUSSELL: Does the money that you win go into your pocket, or does it go to another source?

NASTASE: No. It goes into my wife's pocket.

156

RUSSELL: Another source, in fact!

NASTASE: Yes.

RUSSELL: Right, who's the one person in the world whom you most fear? On a tennis court?

NASTASE: What do you mean?

RUSSELL: Of whom are you most afraid?

NASTASE: Well, I play, all the players, the great tennis players, and the only one which I never beat is Ken Rosewall. And I think it's great—for me it's the best.

RUSSELL: When do you think you will be playing him next?

NASTASE: I don't know. I hope he will play again.

RUSSELL: Well, you've said nice things about England, and about how you'd like to live here, and Wimbledon is now less than a year off, isn't it? It is less than a year to your next visit, to which we look forward with eager anticipation. Good luck in the intervening time. Thank you, Ilie Nastase.

(*applause*)

DAME FLORA MACLEOD

(*bagpipe music; applause*)

RUSSELL: My next guest lives in the oldest inhabited castle in Scotland. It looms out of the mist on the Isle of Skye and there's talk that it's watched over by fairies. She's the undisputed Queen of the castle, because it's the seat of the Clan MacLeod, and she is chief of the Clan. At ninety-five, she's still reputed to walk the mile from her home to church each Sunday and back again. Ladies and gentlemen, Dame Flora MacLeod of MacLeod . . .

(*applause*)

Now, Dame Flora, you live up there in draughty Dunvegan. Do you have a piper to waken you up in the morning?

DAME FLORA: In the old days we did, but in these days it's too difficult. A piper's got to do much more than pipe: he's got to be a gardener, or a forester, or a chauffeur.

RUSSELL: But what do you have for . . . for waking up? Do you have muzak?

DAME FLORA: In the most commonplace way, we wake ourselves up.

(*audience laughter*)

I expect that's what most of you do. Now, I longed to break into Mr Harty and say, when he talked about the fairies, that most certainly fairies play an immensely important part in our history. And when somebody asked my little great-grandson whether he believed in fairies, he said, 'Of course I do. I'm descended from one!'

(*audience laughter*)

RUSSELL: Now, what about your day? The way you spend each day when you're in residence at Dunvegan. Is it all to do with making porridge and drinking whisky?

DAME FLORA: What a question! . . . I thought the whisky-drinking was happening here behind us.

(*audience laughter; applause*)

. . . Do you know what whisky is in Gaelic, in the language of my island? It's called *uisge*, and *uisge* is the Gaelic word for water, and whisky is the water of the Highlands.

158

RUSSELL: Now, you're Chief of your Clan . . .

DAME FLORA: Yes. And that's . . . in a way a terrible thing. Because, of course, we always had men Chiefs, and they had to do the fighting, and there was a tremendous lot of fighting in the olden days. It was largely a question of survival – of having enough food for your clan and your clansmen and their families.

RUSSELL: So . . . you don't do any fighting now?

DAME FLORA: No. And unfortunately our last male heir was killed in the First War, and now you see they've sunk so low as to have a woman.

RUSSELL: Oh, come on . . .! Was there any opposition to your taking that position?

DAME FLORA: No, I think they thought a lot about it and I think they felt rather sad because it was the first time such a thing had happened. But I think they very wisely decided that a woman who lived at Dunvegan in the ancient home and on the old clan lands, the daughter of her father, was really a better choice than saying 'No'.

RUSSELL: You travel extensively round the world visiting other MacLeods?

DAME FLORA: Aren't I lucky? Because I've discovered a great truth, which is that a clan is really a family. The Gaelic word for son is *mac* and the Gaelic word for children is *clan* and if you say 'I am the child of the son of Leod,' surely you're saying 'We are a family,' and the family's scattered all over the world. They've founded homes in all the great English-speaking countries. And they invite me to their homes, and I go and stay with them and I have the most lovely friendships, and they come and stay at Dunvegan.

RUSSELL: But it means that you get to all parts of the world and you have a very good time. You've been recently to the Waldorf Astoria in New York for a thrash-out banquet?

DAME FLORA: Yes, to celebrate my birthday in New York with a great banquet. Well, isn't that fun?

(*audience laughter*)

Don't you think?

RUSSELL: What is going to happen when you're a hundred years old?

DAME FLORA: I shall be under ground, I sincerely hope . . .

(*audience laughter*)

RUSSELL: I have sailed many times past Dunvegan Castle but have never ever been there. Next time I come anywhere near it, can I come and knock upon your door?

DAME FLORA: (*pauses, then turns to audience*) I think he'd much better telephone first.
(*audience laughter*)
RUSSELL: That's the indomitable MacLeod spirit. Dame Flora, thank you very much indeed.
(*applause*)

LULU

RUSSELL: May I again welcome you to the show, and a special welcome to my first guest tonight. She's been described as bubbling, bouncing and cuddly, and several years ago, as the girl any mother would be proud to have as her daughter. But since then, she has come a long way, describing herself, now, as much more mature, and she is here tonight to talk to us. Ladies and gentlemen, the lovely Lulu!

(*music; applause*)

First of all, I may say welcome to you, but secondly, I want to tell you it's going to be a very deep, penetrating, in-depth crucifixion, this interview. I'm really going to go . . .

LULU: Oh well, I'm going to go now.

RUSSELL: No, hold on a minute . . . And therefore I want to begin by asking you the most difficult question I can . . .

LULU: Yes?

RUSSELL: . . . which is, what is it you said that enabled you to win the West of Scotland Burns Recitation Competition?

LULU: Oh God! (*bursting into laughter*) Who told you about that? I think it was 'Ti a Moos' which in English is 'To a Mouse' by Robert Burns, and it was 'Wee sleekit . . .' Do you want me to do a bit for you?

RUSSELL: Yes, can you? Do you have to stand up for it?

LULU: No, I'll sit, I'll sit. I'm much more casual these days.

> '*Wee sleekit, cow'rin' timorous beastie,*
> *O what a panic's in thy breastie!*
> *Thou need na walk awa sae . . .*

I've forgotten it! (*laughs*)

> '*Thou need na walk awa sae hasty*
> *Wi' bickering brattle!*
> *For I wad rin an' chase thee*
> *Wi' murd'ring prattle.*'

(*applause*)

161

RUSSELL: Did anyone understand that at all?

LULU: Well, I certainly didn't. In fact, you know, the teachers used to teach you to say it, and I was always stupidly frightened to ask them what it meant.

RUSSELL: Then you obviously must be a good mimic. I mean, did you mimic, did you imitate, the teacher who taught you that poem?

LULU: Yes, yes.

RUSSELL: Now, you've come a long way from that, haven't you? I mean you've moved a long way forward, and you've just been working with David Bowie?

LULU: That's right, yes.

RUSSELL: How did you come to be doing that?

LULU: Well, David and I were working up in the north of England and we met in this hotel, in the foyer. He was going to do a concert there that night. And it was, 'Oh hallo, how are you? All right?' You know. And we started to talk. And then, after my show, there was a whole gang of people with him, and I had my producer and my assistant with me and we all had drinks, and we were talking, and they were playing the piano, and we started to sing, you know. And he said he'd quite like to record me, and I said, 'That would be a good idea.' That's really how it came about.

RUSSELL: And did you shoot off to France to do that?

LULU: Yes, David was doing 'Pin-Ups' – his album 'Pin-Ups', and I was busy working, rehearsing for a summer season I did last year, but I had two days off, and he said, 'Why don't you come over?' So I did. Went over to France.

RUSSELL: And what's it like? – this fabled château in France? I mean, a lot of people go up there. Elton John goes up there.

LULU: Yes, that's true. Elton John did 'Honky Château' there. And the Stones, I think, have recorded there. It's really fabulous. I can't think of a nicer way to go and record.

RUSSELL: But you all live there, do you?

LULU: You arrive at this beautiful château . . . Well, actually, it's a bit falling-apart really. It's a bit . . . it could do with a good clean.

RUSSELL: You didn't do any dusting while you were there?

LULU: (laughs) No. It could have done with it, though. But it's a very nice way to record, because you stay there. There are lots and lots of bedrooms, and a recording studio, and you record all night and all day. I think you obviously pay for the place, just for a certain amount of days, or weeks when you go to it. In a studio here, you have to pay by the hour, you see.

RUSSELL: Right, but there you book up for . . . B and B and R: bed and breakfast and recording.

Now, on recent shows that I've seen you in, on television, you've been, if you'll forgive me for saying this, much cooler, much less coy than you used to be.

LULU: Am I? That's good. I think that's good, because I have watched myself on television at times, and thought how coy I am. You know? I don't know what it is. I think when people start telling you you're cute, you start believing it. And you think, 'Oh, I'm cute.' And then I'd see myself on television, and I'd think 'Oh my God! You're certainly not cute, you're revolting, you know.' (*laughs*)

I think it's possibly that I'm getting older. And possibly that I have watched myself being cute, and I don't like it.

RUSSELL: You *are* very old, aren't you, now?

LULU: Very, yes. Twenty-five. But I feel much older because I've been in this business for so long. Feels like a long time, you know.

RUSSELL: Well you have, and been successful for a long time.

LULU: Ten years.

RUSSELL: One of the things that you have become is, as in your poem. I mean you're slee . . . I think you are much more 'sleekie'.

LULU: *Sleekit!* No, not . . . (*bursts out laughing*)

RUSSELL: Is that the wrong word?

LULU: I hope you don't mean—do you know what 'sleekit' means?

RUSSELL: I thought 'sleekit' meant 'slinky'.

LULU: Russell, sleekit means . . . kind of devious, I think. A bit devious, yes.

RUSSELL: Oh well, I don't mean that. I don't mean that.

LULU: You mean sleek, do you?

RUSSELL: I meant that you were sleek, slim, svelte, cool, together.

LULU: Ah, that's what I thought you meant.

RUSSELL: Now also, you've obviously changed your mind about certain things. A lot of people in your position get trapped over interviews that they gave a long time back when they say one thing, and then events overtake them. Do you know what I mean by that?

LULU: What do you mean?

RUSSELL: Well, some years ago you were saying that you wouldn't entertain marriage, for instance, and that you wanted to remain chaste and cool.

LULU: That I wouldn't entertain marriage? I said that I wouldn't get married?

RUSSELL: Yes.

163

LULU: Did I say that? I don't remember saying that. I don't actually remember saying that I never wanted to get married.

RUSSELL: Well, somebody must have invented that. What I'm trying to say is that a person as successful as you are obviously is open to a lot of pressure, to a lot of different kinds of pressures, the pressures of success . . . How do you accommodate yourself to those?

LULU: Can you mention something that might be a terrific pressure?

RUSSELL: Well right, I'll mention a few: recognition.

LULU: I like it.

RUSSELL: No pressure?

LULU: I like it. I don't mind.

RUSSELL: Here goes number two: wealth?

LULU: Oh blimey! (*bursts into laughter*) I can cope with that—I mean that's sort of exaggerating. You make money, but you have to spend a lot of money in this business, too. And . . . er, you get taxed a lot, you know.

RUSSELL: Do you enjoy spending money?

LULU: Very much.

RUSSELL: I must say the first time I saw you, I could hardly see you because in fact you were behind mountains of shopping.

LULU: That's right. I had been out for some food and stuff, yes . . .

RUSSELL: Do you enjoy cooking?

LULU: Sometimes. I'm not very good at it, actually.

RUSSELL: But you're a butcher's lass?

LULU: A butcher's lass. Yes. My father used to get the best meat when I was at home in Scotland. He'd bring home maybe liver one day, and the next day it would be steak, and we were fed very well. But the terrible thing was myself, my brother and my mother used to get so fed up with it. And I used to say to my mum, 'I canna have that liver again, Mum. I'd much rather have beans on toast.' And you couldn't tell my father that, you see. He would go mad. He'd say, 'There's people starving in the world, and you're no' eating this good meat.' So, (*whispers*) we used to have to give it to the neighbours and say, 'Don't tell my daddy, whatever you do.' And he'd come home at night, and he'd say, all proud, 'Did you enjoy your liver, then?' 'Oh it was smashing, daddy.'

(*audience laughter*)

Mother used to say, 'God forgive us for telling all these lies. He's going to find us out one of these days.'

RUSSELL: You obviously have a deep affection for your family. I mean, your eyes light up when you are talking about them.

164

Were you determined to leave home?

LULU: I didn't think I was, but my mother said if she hadn't let me go when I was fifteen, she thinks that I would have gone later on.

RUSSELL: Were you determined in the classroom as well?

LULU: Determined not to work. Oh, I was terrible. I was more interested in painting my nails and combing my hair.

RUSSELL: Your nails are very beautiful. What have you got on them?

LULU (*in a 'Mayfair' accent*): Girls, there's red underneath, and then there's a couple of coats of the black with the glitter on the top (*camera close-up*).

RUSSELL: Lulu's nails! Ladies and gentlemen, Lulu's nails!

(*applause*)

Well, let's get back to you briefly in Scotland. Has it turned out as you expected it would have when you left home all those years ago, ten years ago? Has your life turned out as you expected?

LULU: Oh, I never, ever expected to still be in showbusiness when I was twenty-five, and to have been as lucky as I am in my life, with my work and everything. I never even thought about it. I never thought I would be sitting here with Russell Harty, on his show! And talking, and having my own series and records and things like that. You don't imagine anything like that's going to happen.

RUSSELL: Have you ever, in the middle of the night, for instance, after a hell of a bad day, woken up, or not gone to sleep, and said, 'I'm going to chuck the whole thing up, and go back to Scotland?'

LULU: No . . .

RUSSELL: No?

(*audience laughter*)

LULU: Sorry about that (*laughs*).

RUSSELL: I have to tell you, you're one of the most brutally honest people that's ever been sitting here on my show.

LULU: Yes, I think I probably am a bit brutally honest.

RUSSELL: Do you have no illusions at all? I mean, are you as together, and as cool, and as svelte, and . . .

LULU: I love that 'svelte' bit! Say that again.

RUSSELL: . . . non-sleekit, as you appear to be?

LULU (*laughing*): 'Non-sleekit' Oh no, listen, you know – I mean, everybody's got their bad points, but I'm no' tellin' you what they are!

(*audience laughter*)

You have to find them out for yourself. I'm just the same as everybody else, you know, I'm not any more special . . .

165

RUSSELL: You're painting such ridiculous . . . Now come on, Lulu, . . . you're *not* the same as everybody!

LULU: Well, what I mean is, in my nature. I'm not a wonderful human being. I'm just a normal person. I get into bad moods, and I can shout and scream as much as anybody. Probably more. And I think I'm pretty vicious when I'm in a rotten mood. You know, I get a very disgruntled face. But generally, I think I'm probably quite a happy person.

RUSSELL: It's a bit since you had a disc at the top of the charts, isn't it?

LULU: Yes, it is really.

RUSSELL: Does that worry you at all, ever?

LULU: Worries my ego, yes. Upsets my ego terribly. It's nice, you see, to have a hit record. I mean, I can work without having a hit record. It's not that if I don't have the hit I don't get any work. But when you have one it's a real nice boost. It's like a bonus. It's lovely.

RUSSELL: But, there's one sort of creeping its way up now, isn't there? – the Bowie one.

LULU: That's right.

RUSSELL: It's called 'The Man Who Sold The World'.

LULU: Yes.

RUSSELL: How about giving us a flash of it? I mean, I mean. . . .

(*audience laughter*)

LULU: Did you hear that? You heard that, didn't you? Charming!

RUSSELL: While I sit here and stroke this, (*stroking Lulu's hat*) will you sing for us?

LULU: Oh, but I must have my hat, Russell.

RUSSELL: You must have your hat?

LULU: Oh I must, I couldn't sing without it.

RUSSELL: Well, here it is, and here is Lulu with 'The Man Who Sold the World'!

(*applause*)

ARTHUR ASKEY

RUSSELL: Now, this is a special week indeed for my next guest because this week he begins his fiftieth year in show business, and in 1929 the *Daily Mail* said of him: 'He shows symptoms of being able to amuse in a way all his own. He does not dance,' it said, 'but looks as though he could.' Since then he's entertained three generations on stage, screen and radio. Ladies and gentlemen, Mr Arthur Askey.

(*music; applause*)

ARTHUR: Have I aged?

RUSSELL: A bit, a bit.

ARTHUR: Oh, there, you see. I wish I was that side. That's my best side. I'll talk to you this way. Go on.

RUSSELL: It is true, isn't it, that you have appeared many, many times before Royalty?

ARTHUR: Yes, I have.

RUSSELL: They've done one or two sneaky things to you, haven't they? I mean, the Queen in particular, when she was Princess Elizabeth . . .

ARTHUR: Oh yes? Well, the first pantomime that the Queen and Margaret saw . . . they were brought to the Palace Theatre by the Queen (the Queen Mum now) to see *Cinderella*. I was Buttons. I was asked . . .

RUSSELL: What were you wearing?

ARTHUR: A zip.

(*roar of laughter*)

Well, going back to the story, Flo Desmond, the principal boy, and I went up to the Royal Box in the interval to be introduced to the Queen Mum and the two princesses. Dessie was always very flamboyant. She was the Prince of Sylvania in this pantomime, with a cloak and tights – very smart. And, as I say, she over-acted a little bit, you know, and as we got into the Royal Box, she disappeared from sight. She did the curtsey, and I fell over her.

(*audience laughter*)

So that was my first introduction to Royalty. And the following year . . .

167

RUSSELL: You weren't knighted while you were doing . . . ?

ARTHUR: No I wasn't. While I was down there, she couldn't find me. But the following year, they came to His Majesty's Theatre, where we were doing the same pantomime, and we went up in the Royal Box again and the Queen Mother, the Queen as she was then, said: 'Do you remember, Mr Buttons, last year you made your entrance in a laundry basket? The children pulled you on and you took the lid up and stood up.' I said, 'Yes.' She said: 'They did that in their pantomime this year at Windsor Castle.' – And the two young princesses looked as if they'd knocked my gags off, you know. They both went like this. (*He puts his hand to his mouth in a gasp of shock.*) Like Jimmy Tarbuck should do now, but doesn't. Knocking off the material.

(*audience laughter*)

RUSSELL: Did you scowl at the princesses?

ARTHUR: Did I what?

RUSSELL: Scowl. Scowl.

ARTHUR: Well I mean, you know me. Any emergency I'm ready for. I just gave them a dazzling smile . . .

RUSSELL: Now, you're on telly tonight and you've been on telly for a long, long time haven't you. In fact, you were in at the very early days?

ARTHUR: Very early days. I was on in the experimental days with Baird. That's in the early 'thirties.

RUSSELL: That's John Logie Baird.

ARTHUR: John Logie Baird, the man what invented television. Curse the feller! Killed the theatres – which I prefer of course to telly. I like live entertainment.

RUSSELL: Now you've spent a lot of your time playing in the north of England, haven't you? Well, (a), you're from the North and (b), you obviously enjoy going back there to play halls and to do pantomime and to do summer shows there. Is that because you're less well understood south of the Border?

ARTHUR: No, no, NO. You're a young feller, you should know that's a fallacy now. In my early days in showbusiness, there were certain Cockney comedians who couldn't go north of Birmingham; there were certain English comedians who couldn't cross the border to Glasgow and Edinburgh and, we were all 'zoned', you know. Of course, in those days I wasn't on music halls anyway. I was doing concert parties. But since radio came in, and more particularly television, a Scotch comic can come South, a Southern comic can go North, and it doesn't matter.

RUSSELL: When you go back to the North, do you keep an ear to the ground to pick up material for yourself?

ARTHUR (*laughing*): I'm using the same material that I used fifteen years ago. I put me gags in a different order, you see. But when I left Liverpool to join this little concert party in London, I'd never been to London before and they booked me blind. I left an office job in Liverpool at £3 a week to go – I was attracted by £6.10 a week as principal comedian with this little concert party. And we opened at the Electric Theatre, Colchester – forty-nine years ago today, and they said to me: 'We think you're gonna be very good, Arthur, but you must drop that Liverpool accent. You must get rid of your accent and you mustn't talk about Diddy Men or jam butty factories or treacle mines.' Of course, Ken Dodd comes along thirty-odd years later and, through radio and television, they know what he's talking about. But in those days I was doing *missionary* work, you know!

(*audience laughter*)

RUSSELL: Did you wear a big hat with . . .?

ARTHUR: No, I kept me clothes on. I wasn't permissive in those days.

RUSSELL: You were telling me the other day that you were standing once at the end of South Pier at Blackpool and you overheard something going on between a man and . . .

ARTHUR: Ah well, if you play Blackpool, you haven't got to look for material. It's round you all the time. I told you about the two ladies who passed me and I heard one say to the other: 'Hey! That's Arthur Askey.' So the other little one ran down and looked at me. As she came up she said: 'Eeee, he's just like he looks, isn't he?'

(*audience laughter*)

And then there was the other couple at the end of the South Pier. A man and a woman were standing there, just looking out to sea – Morecambe Bay, and she said to him: 'Well, will that be the sea that they go abroad on, then?' It's great, isn't it?

RUSSELL: You couldn't write that.

ARTHUR: No, you couldn't.

RUSSELL: It has been said of you that you are too happy a person to make a big great comedian. I mean, you *are* a big great comedian, but people said in the early days you were too happy a person. I think they thought that to be a great comedian, you ought to have an element of sadness round about you and you ought to play sad things.

ARTHUR: True. I think it was James Agate, who was a very famous theatrical critic when I first hit the West End in musicals. He said that if I had any pathos in my make-up, I could be a great comedian.

169

But I don't want pathos. It hurts me. I don't want pathos at all. I like to be happy. I've always tried to give the impression that I'm being happy and want to make other people happy. I don't want to do (*sings*) 'Don't laugh at me . . .' or anything like that, you know.

RUSSELL: Is there unhappiness at all in your life?

ARTHUR: Well, there is unhappiness at the moment, of course. For my little wife . . . we were married forty-eight years yesterday; she was a typist in an office in Liverpool and I was a clerk and when I decided I'd go on the stage, she encouraged me to do so. I went off for twelve months (we were engaged then), and after doing a concert party at £6.10 a week, then a pantomime at £12 a week, which wasn't bad money in those days, you know, I decided we could get married. So we got married and she came round with me; we lived a very, very happy life.

She was most untheatrical, like I think I am myself. I don't belong to any theatrical organisations at all. I used to do me show, clock off and go home. And that was my life. My wife—I always used to say that she thought I was a burglar. She knew I went out at night to do something, but she wasn't quite sure what it was. When I got my O.B.E. (I must drag that in), I said to my wife: 'Do come along to Buckingham Palace and see me get this.' And she said: 'What time is it?' I said, 'Half past ten.' She said: 'I can't go at half past ten. I've got my work to do. It's all right for the Queen. She's got staff.'

And she meant it. And—well, that was the way we lived. As I say, she was most untheatrical. If I mentioned So-and-so—Danny Kaye, for instance—she'd say, 'Who's that?' 'Oh, a famous comedian, you know.'

But the last three or four years, her memory started to go, and unfortunately she got what is known as pre-senile decay. She's now in a home, in a wonderful home, being beautifully looked after by nuns. We're not Catholics but they are fantastic people. So late in my career, nearly fifty years—well, forty-nine years this week, so don't rush me. I've got another year before the fiftieth.

RUSSELL: You're *entering* your fiftieth year.

ARTHUR: That's a good boy. And I'm a Presbyterian.

(*audience laughter*)

What I mean to say is, we were getting to the point where we were thinking of retirement. At least *I* was. And particularly when her memory started to go, and I thought we should go and live out in the country or something like that. But it didn't work out that way. And the doctor said to me, 'Well, the only thing to keep you sane is to keep on working,' and thanks to the great British public and kind friends that I've got, I'm still very much in demand. And I can still keep going on.

RUSSELL: Indeed you are. Lots of luck and lots of success to you. (*applause*)

EDNA EVERAGE

(ALIAS BARRY HUMPHRIES)

RUSSELL: Now, Edna Everage, I understand, has now arrived fresh from the première of her first film which opened in London last night. Please come in, Mrs Edna Everage . . .

(*music; applause*)

EDNA EVERAGE: Hello, Simon—you know I'm *here*, darling. Bless you . . .!

RUSSELL: And how are you?

EDNA EVERAGE: Very, very well indeed and all the better for seeing you, pet, you little lamb! (*to the audience*) How do you do, everybody? It's a very, very exciting occasion for me . . . May I sit down, please, Simon?

RUSSELL: Please sit down, yes.

EDNA EVERAGE: (*sighs*) Oh dear! Oh goodness, look at these people!

RUSSELL: You've just come fresh from your première?

EDNA EVERAGE: Oh, it has been *such* an exciting week, and a very exciting fortnight for Australia it's been too, Simon—the Opera House and all these marvellous things that have been happening, the Australian Ballet . . .

RUSSELL: Could I just say that my name is Russell? Russell is my name.

EDNA EVERAGE: I don't know why you bothered to change it, dear. We've forgiven you (*whoops of laughter*) . . . We have! You haven't done anything wrong, darling, but I'll call you Russell. It's a very Australian name as a matter of fact . . .

RUSSELL: Is it?

EDNA EVERAGE: Are you an Australian?

RUSSELL: Only on my mother's side.

EDNA EVERAGE: I thought there might have been a little bit of Australian blood there . . . because you are so wonderfully natural. Oh, what can we chat about?

RUSSELL: Could we talk about the film?

EDNA EVERAGE: (*taking no notice*) . . . And these gloves of course are wonderful, darling. They are! Those of you who haven't got

172

colour television, they are a beautiful shade of silver – and I don't know, they're very gentle and very kind to my hands. But they are made of a sort of – I think a derivative of Brillo pad. And do you know, I do not tell a lie, Russell, if I may call you that . . .

RUSSELL: Yes, please do.

EDNA EVERAGE: I pop these on first thing in the morning, because they are just very slightly abrasive, and I run over my legs with them . . .

(*audience outburst*)

. . . I do! Because they are a wonderful depilatory, they are, and I do my upper lip and everything before I put on my base. Oh, we women have our little secrets, we do!

RUSSELL: You er. . . .

EDNA EVERAGE: I always feel relaxed on this programme because they're such a lovely friendly audience you have too. Aren't they lovely? So many young people, too. I'm very excited, because not only of course have I been to see my own film, *The Adventures of Barry MacKenzie*, at the Columbia in Shaftesbury Avenue, but I've been going to see a lot of other films, and particularly my interest was aroused by Mr Zeffirelli. Because I think the more we stars see of other people's work . . .

(*audience laughter*)

. . . I popped up to Swiss Cottage to the Odeon there and there was a very interesting programme: *Ten Rillington Place* and *There's a Girl in My Soup* in the same programme.

RUSSELL: That's called out of the frying pan into the fire.

EDNA EVERAGE: (*laughs*) Your English humour . . .

RUSSELL: Before . . .

EDNA EVERAGE: Now *I'm* doing all the talking . . .

RUSSELL: Well yes . . .

EDNA EVERAGE: . . . and I'm not giving you a chance to say anything and . . .

RUSSELL: You . . .

EDNA EVERAGE: . . . it *is* your programme, don't forget that, dear.

(*audience laughter*)

You mustn't, you're so self-effacing. I've watched you with all those wonderful people – was it Elsa Lanchester? I saw you with her . . . Pearl Bailey – isn't she *marvellous*? I think she is. A contented person . . .

RUSSELL: Hold on a minute, let me be Canute for a moment and stem your tide, because we've been talking a lot about you . . . Now

Australia . . . Australia is redolent with history at this moment isn't it?

EDNA EVERAGE: Now I have been of course in two dilemmas at the moment. First of all I have come over for the première of the film . . .

RUSSELL: Right.

EDNA EVERAGE: . . . and so missed the official opening of the Sydney Opera House which was a great blow, but I want to stay on in England, particularly of course for the 14th November, for Princess Anne's wedding, because that is a very, very wonderful moment and I'm . . . you never know what, I just might get a little invitation. I hear that . . .

(*audience laughter*)

. . . It's possible. And of course, the gifts . . . I suppose she has left a list at Marshall and Snelgrove . . .

(*audience laughter*)

. . . But I don't know what to give her, I want to give her something a little bit unusual, Russell . . .

RUSSELL: Right.

EDNA EVERAGE: At the moment I'm . . . I'm torn between her window and her toilet. I thought, at first, it would be a lovely thought and a very Australian gift to give her – a bandicoot fur toilet cosy . . .

(*audience laughter*)

. . . and then I thought, no – I thought no, that's a little bit . . .

RUSSELL: A what? Say it slowly.

EDNA EVERAGE: Bandicoot. That's one of our marsupials. A bandicoot fur toilet cosy. That's for popping over the seat. You know that?

RUSSELL: Yes.

EDNA EVERAGE: Because it takes the chill off it. And . . .

(*audience laughter*)

. . . also I thought perhaps a venetian blind, because venetian blinds are very, very Australian and she is in that rarity of all English homes – a detached home. She is.

RUSSELL: Yes.

EDNA EVERAGE: So I thought a venetian blind there because she can peep through it and see who's coming up the drive.

(*audience uproar*)

. . . And, of course – she won't want *every* Tom, Dick and Harry coming in the front door – well, certainly not in the first few weeks of her marriage. And so she'll have that to peep through . . .

RUSSELL: You mean when she moves to Sandhurst?

EDNA EVERAGE: Well, if she *does* move, if her family say 'All right' about that. I know how it is—I've got daughters and a wonderful family at home, you know.

RUSSELL: Do you worry for their sakes?

EDNA EVERAGE: Well, I'm a little bit—not so worried about Kenny of course because he can look after himself, and my daughter Valmae of course is married and my son Brucie. I'm worried about my husband at the moment. He's all on his own, and I suppose I should be toddling back to Melbourne. But then of course there's this wonderful Opera House now. There's been a lot of laughter. I noticed, when it was mentioned this evening, Russell, there was a little—it has to be admitted—a little gale of laughter amongst these folk here.

RUSSELL: A little gale . . . ?

EDNA EVERAGE: No, there is a certain amount of laughter about the time the Opera House took to build.

RUSSELL: Well, it took forever, didn't it?

EDNA EVERAGE: Well, be that as it may, Rome was not built in a day, dear.

(*audience laughter*)

—It wasn't, and they were following a Danish plan.

(*audience laughter*)

They can be very, very tricky. But on my travels I recently went to Athens. Have you been there, dear?

RUSSELL: No, no.

EDNA EVERAGE: It's a fascinating place. And in Athens . . .

RUSSELL: Is it redolent with history?

EDNA EVERAGE: It is redolent with history and redolent with many other things too, I can tell you.

(*audience laughter*)

. . . But when I was in Athens, I noticed they've got a great big hill and it's called the Parthenon Hill. And on the top of it, right on the top of it, is their . . . Opera House! Now Russell, that was started *thousands* of years ago, and it isn't finished *yet*.

(*audience laughter*)

. . . and it hasn't even got a roof on it, dear. And they've got the cheek to put it on their brochures too. Isn't that typical? Isn't that typical of them, darling? This is a little poem that I have written if I may take up the time of your viewers.

RUSSELL: Is it in honour of anything?

EDNA EVERAGE: Well, it is really in honour of the triumph not only of this wonderful film which will be running for goodness-knows-how-many days at the Columbia, Shaftesbury Avenue, but also the

Australian Ballet and oh – everyone.

RUSSELL: Sir Robert Helpmann?

EDNA EVERAGE: Sir Robert Helpmann. Isn't he wonderfully well preserved?

(*audience laughter*)

. . . Anyway, this is just a little bit about Australia and I'd like to read it as a little tribute, if I may:

> In the world of success and failure,
> Have you noticed the genius spark
> Seems brightest in folk from Australia?
> We all leave an indelible mark.
> You just have to go to the opera,
> Or an art-show, or glance at your shelves
> To see in a trice that Australians
> Have done *terribly* well for themselves.

(*audience laughter*)

> Joan Sutherland, Rupert Murdoch, Scobie Breasley
> Have all pitted themselves against the Pom,
> And the cultural race they've won easily
> In spite of the land they come from.
> Wilfred Thomas, Germaine Greer, Hammond Innes –
> To mention a few famous names –
> Have all taken to Old England's bosom
> Along with Skippy and Mr Clive James . . .

(*audience laughter*)

> . . . Did you know that Rolf Harris was Australian?
> . . . Peter Finch, Coral Browne, Keith Michell,
> All your best dentists come from the land of the gum,
> And they've all done so terribly well.
> Evonne Goolagong hails from the outback,
> The white hope of Australian sport.
> I could sing out our praises all evening
> And my list would be still far too short.
> You may ask me with ill-disguised envy
> Why we Aussies get all the right breaks.
> So here is my recipe for world-wide renown:
> Mother's love, lots of sun, *juicy steaks*!

(*audience applause*)

RUSSELL: Well, after all this fame that's falling all over you with films and Sydney and God knows what, are you going to remain a superstar or are you going back to Moonee Ponds?

176

EDNA EVERAGE: My place—I feel—is in the bosom of my family, Russell . . . But not yet!

RUSSELL: When you make a sequel to the film you've just made, and when you come back to launch it on an unsuspecting Europe . . .

EDNA EVERAGE: You're being a little bit satirical, I think, there . . .

RUSSELL: Will you come back and talk about the next great triumph?

EDNA EVERAGE: I'd love to, because I just feel at home. I feel relaxed talking to you. You could be my son . . .

(*audience laughter*)

RUSSELL: Well, Mother, thank you very much.

EDNA EVERAGE: Isn't he gorgeous? No wonder you're still clinging on to your programme. I think it's wonderful, don't you?

(*audience outburst*)

. . . Thank you.

RUSSELL: Edna Everage breaking us all up. She looks remarkably like Barry Humphries. That's all we have time for this week. Goodnight.

EDNA EVERAGE: Goodbye, dears. Bye now!

(*applause*)

NOEL
Charles Castle

'The book is witty and sparkles just like a Coward script and is enhanced by contemporary photographs, playbills, cartoons, lyrics, and scores from some of Noel's well known songs. A remarkable book about a very remarkable man.'
North Western Evening Mail
£1.50 *Illustrated*

AS TIME GOES BY
Derek Taylor

'An episodic account of Taylor's life and times and ranges from early journalistic chores, like covering council meetings, to his days as Brian Epstein's personal assistant and three years in America publicising pop stars and people like Mae West.'
Evening Standard

75p *Illustrated*

MICK JAGGER
J. Marks

An original and powerful portrait of one of the most phenomenal performers of our age.

60p *Illustrated*

BLACK ELK SPEAKS
The life Story of a Holy Man of the Oglala Sioux as told to John G. Neihardt.

'A beautiful and eloquent testament to the dream of a way of life that died with a people in defeat.'
The Cork Examiner

90p *Illustrated*

THE CONQUEST OF THE INCAS
John Hemming

'Much the best book on the Incas since Presott's, which it is entitled to supersede.'
Sunday Times

£1.75 *Illustrated*

GERONIMO
His Own Story
Edited by S. M. Barrett

'Fact, folklore, anger, humour, tragedy and history are generously blended in this chronicle.'
Wall Street Journal

65p Illustrated

SEXUAL POLITICS
Kate Millett

'The seminal book in the struggle for Women's Rights. Supremely interesting . . . brilliantly conceived.'
New York Times

60p

ONE DIMENSIONAL MAN
Herbert Marcuse

'A "classic" of social criticism . . . The analysis he presents is impressive without doubt . . . for the ferocity and power with which he reveals the pervasive alienation and un-freedom of modern technological society.'
Peace News

75p

THE PRIMAL SCREAM
Arthur Janov

'Several times a century a book appears which holds promise of reshaping society . . . One such book has just been released which in the field of psychology could wield as much influence as the early writings of Sigmund Freud and probably work to a much better end.'
Berkeley Gazette

95p

THE BOOK OF THE DAMNED
Charles Fort

The Book of the Damned records over 1000 events of the most mysterious and provoking character that have occurred in the world on which science has remained strangely silent . . . 'No other book has so filled me with wonder, speculation and excitement.'
Taylor Caldwell

75p

THE FLYING SAUCER VISION
John Michell

'We have no hesitation in recommending this illustrated well-written and well-produced book as a successful example of the results of research into the mythological past and an awareness of the present day pattern of flying saucer visitation.'
Orbit

60p *Illustrated*

THE LIFE BEYOND DEATH
Arthur Ford

'*The Life Beyond Death* will hold one's interest from start to finish. It is a fascinating and thought-provoking book which will be discussed long after the final chapter has been reached.'
Cork Examiner

75p

THE PARADE'S GONE BY . . .
Kevin Brownlow

The classic and acclaimed work on Holywood during the 'golden age' between 1912 and the advent of sound sixteen years later.

£1.75 *Illustrated*

STANLEY KUBRICK DIRECTS
Alexander Walker

Richly illustrated with over 350 stills, which add force to the detailed analyses of style and content, this book traces the flow of Kubrick's work from *Paths of Glory* to *Dr Strangelove*, *2001: A Space Odyssey*, and *A Clockwork Orange*.

£1 *Illustrated*

POETRY DIMENSION [1]
Edited by Jeremy Robson

'It *really* is an annual of the best poetry, and prose about poetry, published in books and magazines during the past year . . . It adds up to a lively record of what has been going on among those whose work is the setting down of the best words in the best order. No public library should be without a copy.'
The Times

75p

MUNBY
Man of Two Worlds
Derek Hudson

'Quite apart from the absorbing story of Hannah and "Massa" and the compassionate insight into the conditions of working women, Munby's diaries offer the bonus of a full social calendar. Their story is a unique and compelling document which extends our knowledge not only of Victoriana but of human behaviour at its most honourable.'
Spectator

£1.60 *Illustrated*

THE BOOK ON THE TABOO AGAINST KNOWING WHO YOU ARE
Alan Watts

'This lovely and humerous work will shock, outrage, excite, delight and profoundly stimulate anyone who has ever asked "Who or What am I?".'
Irish Press

45p

WORLDS IN COLLISION
Immanuel Velikovsky

'Fascinating . . . in its stupendous pictures of a world in the grip of cosmic forces, in its parallels drawn from the annals of the ancients in many lands, and in its vast implications.'
Oxford Mail

60p